PERSONS IN COMMUNION

Patriarch Athenagoras Orthodox Institute
Distinguished Lecture Series
2000

Persons in Communion: A Theology of Authentic Relationships

Kyriaki Karidoyanes FitzGerald

InterOrthodox Press
Berkeley, California

© Kyriaki Karidoyanes FitzGerald, 2006
Published by InterOrthodox Press
Patriarch Athenagoras Orthodox Institute
2311 Hearst Avenue
Berkeley, California 94709

ISBN 1-932401-08-3

All rights reserved.

Library of Congress Cataloging-in-Publication Data
FitzGerald, Kyriaki Karidoyanes, 1956-
Persons in Communion : a theology of authentic relationships / Kyriaki Karidoyanes FitzGerald.
   p. cm. -- (Distinguished lecture series ; 2000)
  ISBN 1-932401-08-3 (alk. paper)
1. Interpersonal relations--Religious aspects--Orthodox Eastern Church. 2. Women in the Orthodox Eastern Church. 3. Orthodox Eastern Church--Doctrines. I. Title. II. Series: Distinguished lectures (Patriarch Athenagoras Orthodox Institute) ; 2000.
     BX323.F58 2006
    233--dc22   2006002062

*To Thomas:
My friend, teacher, hero,
and beloved husband*

CONTENTS

Preface ... ix

I. Persons in Communion
  1. Aspects of Orthodox Anthropology:
    An Introduction ... 1

  2. The Holy Trinity:
    Persons in Relationship ... 9

  3. The Human Person in Relationship:
    Some Corollary Affirmations ... 23

  Appendix: Observations on
  Authentic Relationships: A Therapist's Revelation ... 75

II. Looking Toward the Future:
    The Ministries of Women ... 77

  Appendix: Church of Greece Restores
  Diaconate for Women ... 117

About the Patriarch Athenagoras Orthodox Institute ... 120

Orthodox Christianity has much, much more to offer the contemporary world. In Orthodoxy, one can find not only the correct faith in the true God but also the correct perception of humankind as the image of God, of the world, and of creation.

His All Holiness Ecumenical Patriarch
Bartholomew of Constantinople
Enthronement Address
November 2, 1991

Preface

Between the pages and lines of every book, there lie stories that sustain them. In the case of this work, four vivid early memories as well as a few recent ones come to mind.

The first memory concerns the person of my spiritual father and professor Fr. Maximos Aghiorgoussis (now Metropolitan Maximos of Pittsburgh). During my seminary studies at Hellenic College and Holy Cross Greek Orthodox School of Theology, he served as professor of Orthodox Dogmatic Theology. He is regarded as one of the most respected Orthodox theologians today. I remember in particular the gentle gaze of his attention as he patiently listened to me, whenever I would seek his help. It was as if he was holding me in quiet spiritual embrace before the loving God, all the while holding me accountable to Him. Even now many, many others also are benefiting from his witness and ministry. Any healthy theological and/or spiritual service I may have come to offer later in life (including my marriage!), would never have occurred if it was not for his intercession, spiritual direction and teaching. In his person, through his prayer and pastoral care, through his course instruction and high scholarly standards, Fr. Maximos taught and is still teaching me that personal integrity of heart, thought and action before God, one's self, others and creation, within the ebb and flow of our daily relationships is our ultimate concern.

The second memory concerns the relationship my husband and I had with my Orthodox Dogmatic Theology professor from the School of Theology of the University of Thessaloniki, Fr. John Romanides of blessed memory. Having formerly taught at Holy Cross, he was also our "home town" connection while we were studying in Greece during the late 1970's. It was after I had successfully completed the necessary coursework for a doctorate in dogmatic theology under Fr. John's academic direction, when he later said to me privately and to many in public seminar lectures: *"…in order for our dogmatic theology to be real, it must be pastoral; it has to give life!"* His assertion of "Orthodox fact" has become the cornerstone of my subsequent labor both personal, as well as academic.

The third memory related to this topic is for some reason, more faded and imprecise. I remember during my early months of doctoral study at Boston University, standing to one side of the School of Theology main door one late rainy afternoon, waiting for my husband. During this particularly gray day, the Professor of Ethics, Dr. Paul Deats, was busily heading out of the building from another direction. Nevertheless, he noticed me, veered toward me and stopped to say "hello." Together with Professors Harell Beck, Horace Allen, John Cartwright and Homer Jernigan, who later became my advisor and deeply cherished mentor, Paul Deats was very kind to me throughout my course of doctoral studies. Today as I write this, I wonder if he and they were watching out for me in some small way. I shake my head now in disbelief, thinking this may be the case. If this is so, at this very moment I am more than a little bit suspicious of my beloved former dean and professor, Fr. Stanley Harakas, also a graduate of Boston University, who may have put them up to this. I will be forever indebted to him as well as to them, as their compassion certainly abetted me through lengthy spells of overwhelming isolation that sometimes comes with Ph.D. studies. Perhaps I was never as alone as I felt during those times.

As we entered into a conversation, Paul asked me where my academic interests lay. I remember brightly, yet earnestly, responding with something like: "I think my interests lie at the crossroads of theology and authentic personhood."

I was barely able to say these words when he shot back: "You know, we already tried that back in the seventies and we've moved on from there."

Paul then looked at his watch, seemed surprised by the lapse of time and quickly rushed off, looking back over his shoulder to say "good-bye." Paul's abrupt and possibly annoyed reaction caught me off-guard. Nevertheless, even while taken aback, I realized that a great deal of what was important for me as an Orthodox regarding "theology and authentic relationships" probably was missing from this allegedly completed area of inquiry. As for Paul, our paths only rarely crossed after that day. In some ways, much of this little book is a sincere effort to continue our conversation.

The fourth memory is a flashback to the time my husband and I lived in Geneva, Switzerland where for several years he served as Executive Director of Program Unit I of the World Council of Churches. It was during a meeting of the Unit I Commission when he asked me if I would accompany Metropolitan John Zizioulas to the airport. Metropolitan John served as the Moderator of the Unit I Commission. Unfortunately, he had to leave the meeting early for another commitment.

I first came to know of Metropolitan John's work toward the very end of my studies at Boston University, through his seminal work, *Being as Communion*. The result of painstaking research and incisive examination, this groundbreaking book addressed the Orthodox theological understanding of personhood and related this to issues associated with ecclesiology. Over time, my husband and I developed a warm relationship with Fr. John and our paths crossed at theological conferences and ecumenical events, as well as meetings at our Patriarchate.

Our ride to the airport was pleasant and uneventful. It was only after the metropolitan checked his luggage when we heard the announcement stating his flight was delayed an extra four hours due to air traffic congestion. I invited Fr. John for a light lunch as we waited for his flight.

Once I was sure he was beginning to relax and enjoy his luncheon choice, I naturally took advantage of the opportunity and began to ask him questions about the responses he had been receiving over the years regarding his book. He discussed quite candidly certain critical reactions to his work, as well as changes in relationships with others as appreciation for the material addressed within the volume spread. During our conversation, despite the increased lunchtime hubbub at the airport, our table somehow had become a remarkably quiet and tranquil spot, at least for me. I do not know if the metropolitan noticed this. I asked him if he would describe what it was like writing such a uniquely compelling theological treatise.

With some hesitation, he began very quietly. "You see, Kyriaki...," he stopped to collect his thoughts. At this point in the discussion, his tone and facial expression projected a subtle, self-effacing impression, "I am not a very good writer."

When asked to clarify what he meant by this he responded, "You see, it is as if every piece of information I would study, I would take my pen, dip it in that information and place it deeply, ... very deeply into my mind where it remains for a long time ... before it comes out. This is a very slow process and takes a very long time."

As respectfully as possible, I asked, "Father, do you really mean that something far more is actually occurring when you write than by what your words on the surface seem to be saying right now?"

He pushed himself away from the table slightly and nods in silence. Even while vividly recalling how easily "fools rush in where angels fear to tread," I continued, "please forgive me as I ask you this, Father, are you perhaps referring to prayer?"

At this point, he appears to be looking at me with great tenderness and some vulnerability. "Father, ... did you pray your way through writing the book, ... through every bit of information that you took in?" The thought occurred to me in that instant that perhaps every sentence he wrote in his study may have been mysteriously transfigured by the loving God, Himself, due in large part to his prayer.

Fr. John nodded in the affirmative. "This is why it takes me so long," he replied.

I do not remember much beyond that point of our time together. I hope that I do not embarrass him too much by recounting publicly this small part of our personal conversation and earnestly seek his forgiveness here. Our dialogue that day, which continued on other occasions, became a life-changing event for me. Once again, an unexpected and undeserved surprise encounter presented itself, pointing to the mystery of how theology must give life in order to be real. Theology must give life, as it serves the Author of Life. Even as the human author creates, he or she is called to be in honest relationship with God throughout the entire inquiry. This has profound, resonating ramifications in every aspect of life: our relationship with God, ourselves, one another, and creation. We are changed with every encounter.

Several of the persons I have mentioned in these memories are still with us. Others are not. Yet, somehow, I find them all here with me as I write. From my perspective (even if this is not objectively true!), I was the one initially reaching out to encounter these strangers, at least at first. Experientially, it is another entirely different phenomenon to submit yourself to the encounter of a stranger; a stranger who reaches out to you, befriends you and invites you into his home.

This is essentially, what happened to me through the person of Professor Paul Manolis. On behalf of the Patriarch Athenagoras Orthodox Institute, as the Institute's Director, he invited me to offer the Distinguished Lecture Series for the Fall of 2000. Never would I have ever imagined being honored in this way. He desired this to be the first Distinguished Lecture Series to engage directly theological issues as to that point it had largely focused on historical topics. This caused me to experience a double helping of honor and anxiety. My personal insecurities were unfounded, as my husband and I received exceptionally warm hospitality from the Institute. Words of thanks to the Women's Board, and especially to its President, Jenny Cladis, and two of its members, Virginia Lagiss and Loula Anaston, are not enough. Through their welcome and personal encouragement, they helped quell the fears of this stranger.

During our visit, my joy was raised to an even higher degree. I was able to observe Professor John Klentos working with students and others associated with the Institute. He demonstrated in a subtle, yet powerful and life-giving manner, a deep love and respect for his students. At the same time, he relentlessly held them accountable to a high standard of academic inquiry. I knew John during his studies at Holy Cross and closely followed his work after graduation. Seeing him serve in this manner reminded me of what a noteworthy and gifted person he is, appreciating even more so, the far-sighted vision of those who sought out John to join the Graduate Theological Union and Institute faculty!

The Institute most generously gave me all the time I needed to rewrite my presentations. This text now responds to the subsequent warm and animated lengthy discussions with Paul Manolis that followed. Nevertheless, I never dreamed that personal and health related delays would distract me from completing this commitment until after his retirement! And, so today, I find myself deeply moved as I work together with the current Director of the Institute, my friend, Professor Tony Vrame, whom I knew also as a student and as the former Managing Editor of Holy Cross Orthodox Press. Truly, we must praise God for the decades of labor and wisdom that have brought about the Institute's successes to this point facilitated, in particular, through Paul's vision and leadership. Likewise, with Tony now serving as Director, many future blessings are happily anticipated, as these will in no small part be brought about through his extremely capable collaborative style of servant-leadership.

At this point, I wish to thank former Institute staff persons Natalie Kulukundis and Nancy Haritatos, who helped us in many ways during our stay at Berkeley. Furthermore, profound gratitude is expressed here to Barbara Harris, Stephanie Yazge, Hilary Chala, Soula Mellos, and Lia Lewis (each in her own way, a faithful steward of good theology!) for reviewing drafts of this text. While this was written partially in response to the lengthy discussions that followed each of the lectures, I foresee the possibility of fresh concerns emerging from this modest work. Some preliminary responses to the final draft suggest that writing a follow-up book may need to be considered at some point in the future.

For the reader who has applied extreme long-suffering kindness to bear with me to this point, I wish to thank you! I will end here with the declaration that "reality" is at all times, all about the same thing: Reality consists of all of us and everything abiding in the loving presence of the Living God (cf. Eph. 4:6)). Because we Orthodox Christians firmly hold this to be true, it must also be re-affirmed here that we already are intimately connected to one another through the love of the triune God. Despite the seemingly insurmountable trials of life, even at this very moment, none of us is ever alone. An invisible "cloud of witnesses," (Heb. 12:1) the communion of the saints, who share His love for us, surround each one of us. They share this love with us in countless ways, perhaps not unlike the care extended to me by the compassionate professors mentioned earlier. Mysteriously, they are watching out for us while holding us in their tender care. They extend their and His love for us, as we strive to reach out to the Triune One-Who-Is … as well as one another, all in the presence of everything and everyone that is holy, cradled in the sweet embrace of the love of the living God.

Kyriaki Karidoyanes FitzGerald, Ph.D.
Monday June 12, 2006
The Feast of the Holy Spirit

I

Persons in Communion

Chapter 1

Aspects of Orthodox Anthropology: An Introduction

Jesus Christ in Relationship

The life of Jesus Christ as recorded in the Gospels shows us that He was a person in relationships. He spoke often about His relationship with the Father and the Holy Spirit. He affirmed that He came to do the will of the Father. Through His words and deeds, Jesus revealed to us the loving and merciful Father. At the same time, our Lord also spoke about His relationship with the Spirit. He began His preaching by declaring that the Spirit was upon Him. He spoke about the Spirit as the Comforter and Advocate. He said that He would send the Spirit, who proceeds from the Father, upon His followers. As we shall see, the Lord revealed to us not only the Triune God but also some valuable aspects of the intimate relationship between Himself and the Father and the Spirit.

Throughout His ministry on earth, Jesus also entered into relationship with others. His life was lived in fellowship with others. He called men and women to be His friends and followers. Regardless of their background, occupation, race or gender, Christ invited them to follow Him and to be bearers of His ministry of reconciliation. He united these followers into a community of faith, which is the Church.

Often, Christ challenged the social and religious customs of His day that prevented genuine relationships among persons or diminished the true dignity of the person. For those who turned to Christ in trust, He established a bond of love with Himself and with others. This authentic relationship of love was healing, comforting and inspiring. He spoke of this intimate relationship as the link between the vine and the branches (Jn. 15:1f). As we shall see, our Lord bore witness to the importance of relationships not only with God but also with one another and with all of creation.

Our Lord also lived in relationship with the creation around Him. The physical world became a means through which He revealed Himself and His authority. Let us remember that the faith of the Church is centered upon the bold affirmation that "the Word became flesh and dwelt among us" (Jn. 1:14). Christ is the Word of God who fully entered into human life. He did not disdain the physical world for it was fashioned through Him in the beginning. Indeed, He began His public ministry following His baptism in the water of the Jordan River. He used the wine at the wedding in Cana to perform His first miracle, a true sign of His divine authority. The loaves and fish, the dust of the earth, the waters of the Sea of Galilee, and the hem of His garment became vehicles of His divine activity. He spoke about the birds of the air and the dogs with Lazarus. At the Last Supper, He thankfully took bread and wine, identified it with His own body and blood, and directed His followers to do the same. Throughout His ministry, our Lord bore witness to the importance of relationships with the physical world. He bore witness to the fact that the physical world is truly a gift from God.

Authentic Relationships

Relationships are essential not only to Christian life but to all of human life. With the example of the Lord in mind, we need to recognize that everything depends upon relationships, most especially our relationship with God. Our very existence is an expression of the creative act of God who establishes a fundamental relationship with each of us and with the entire creation. Human life and holiness are rooted in intimate and authentic relationships with God, our true self, others, and the creation. We exist because of the mystery of divine creation. Our relationship with our Creator is central to our identity as human persons.

From the very first moment of our existence, we are involved in many relationships, although we may not be completely aware of this fact. We did not make ourselves! Likewise, we are also in relationship with our human mother who offers her body to provide the environment that sustains us until it is time to be born. Even in the womb, we are in a truly mysterious relationship with the divine, the human, and the material world. We are part of a web of relationships from the very moment of our personal existence. These relationships become more obvious and more visible after our birth. As we grow, we become more affected by all those who enter into a mysterious communion with us, even if we are not fully aware of these relationships and their meaning. Our parents, other family members, and numerous persons begin to touch our lives, and we touch theirs. We are affected by these relationships and we affect others. In addition, we are in relationship with the physical world about us. We do not exist in some sort of void. We exist within the matrix of life in the creation which is a matrix of relationships.

Relationships are not static. They are dynamic. They are meant to develop in a positive and authentic manner. These positive relationships humanize us and deepen our connection with God and others. It is through authentic relationships that we truly become our "self."

Sometimes this call to growth is obvious. For example, we may immediately think of our relationship with our adult family members, our children, our friends. We even have relationships with our pets, who become "members of the family." We may have "relationship" with our garden, knowing its needs and what makes it grow and bloom. These may seem so natural and necessary. At other times, this call to growth in authentic relationship is more subtle. We become caught up in relationships without being consciously aware of their impact or significance, for example, our relationship with teachers. Usually, authentic relationships develop gradually and mysteriously, sometimes with little thought or plan. Think for a moment of the relationships that develop among good friends and trusted neighbors. There is much we take for granted in life that is founded upon and expressed through authentic relationships.

There is a powerful African saying: "I am because you are, and because we are I am." The saying reminds us of the importance of authentic relationships. These words could be applied to our relationship with God. Indeed, the words can also be applied to our relationship with one another. The words remind us that our personal identity is intimately connected with the "other." We do not grow as persons apart from our relationships with others but together and through our relationships.

We could be so bold as to say that the whole cosmos depends upon "authentic relationships." This is so because the very foundation of reality is the mystery of the Triune God who abides in eternity in loving relationship as three divine persons. We Christians profess our faith in the Holy Trinity. We confess *one* God in *three* persons – Father, Son and Holy Spirit. In so doing, we declare that the Triune God is a community of persons. These persons are in a constant state of relationship with each other. At the same time, the divine persons are in relationship with us and the whole creation.

We human persons, created in the "image and likeness" (Gen. 1:27) of this same Trinitarian God, are called to grow in authentic relationship with God, with our own selves, with other persons, and with the creation. With this bold affirmation, we recognize that we are not meant to be autonomous and self-centered individuals. To live in this manner is, ultimately, contrary to our basic human nature that is rooted in the reality of the Triune God. We are meant to be persons in relationship. Indeed, it is only through authentic relationship that we truly become our most true selves and give glory to God. This means that genuine human life must be lived in relationships that are loving, nurturing and healing.

We know, however, that not all relationships are truly authentic and life giving. Not all aid us in our emotional and spiritual growth, or our well-being. Some of us may have a false relationship with our own self. We may live our lives with a "mask" that distorts our true identity and presents a false self to others. We may even lie to our own selves in order to protect this false identity and hence, we develop a false relationship with reality.

Some of us may have a false relationship with God. We may choose to live apart from and in isolation from the True, Living God. Turning from our Heavenly Father, we can choose lesser substitutes that become destructive idols in our life.

We may also find ourselves in destructive relationships with others. Such relationships may lead not only to spiritual and psychological pain but also to physical harm. These unhealthy relationships are not rooted in love. They do not affirm or enhance our truest identity as valuable daughters and sons of God.

And finally, we may not express a healthy relationship with the Creation. We can fall victim to a mentality that abuses the Creation and squanders the natural resources in a selfish and self-centered manner.

Relationships: Given, Broken and Healed

When people come to me seeking spiritual direction or through my work as a pastoral counselor or psychologist, I have found that in one way or another they are attempting to respond to something that needs healing in their lives. Usually, this relates to a disturbance in their everyday functioning that they perceive needs attention. While we all experience the ups and downs of life, they sense that something is not quite right. This is a feeling that all of us can have from time to time.

Sometimes, the conscious reason for reaching out for assistance is very specific. It may be a concern over one's relationship with God. Some people may feel alienated from God. Or, it may be a concern over a relationship with another person or group of persons that is compromising one's feelings, thinking and actions in the present. It is an unhealthy relationship. Still, in other instances, the concern may be rooted in a trauma or series of traumas, losses, addictions, compulsions, moods, or illnesses that take on a life of their own. Eventually, in too many situations, it seems as if the identified issue's toxicity contaminates virtually every other aspect of life. There is a painful sense that our inner life is simply not right.

People also often come seeking something "other" or "more" in their lives. This may be experienced as a kind of low-grade depression, or a subtle, unyielding uneasiness, or a chronic emptiness. It is often expressed as a personal search for meaning and purpose. These persons sense that their life must have greater significance and meaning. This typically is expressed in a direct quest to know God better or to bring a more profound meaning to their life through service to others.

While every case is unique, people usually come hoping to improve their life and to find the "something more" for their life. This is a very positive concern! They are the courageous persons who are willing to truly look at their life and their relationships! They have enough courage to want to examine their life for the sake of growth and improvement. These persons may then invite me to assist them in some small way as they begin more deeply to explore the mystery of their own life in the presence of the loving God.

In one way or another, the symptoms identified indicate that these persons are encountering a breakdown of authentic relationships. Relationships may become wounded or broken in numerous and sometimes very subtle ways. In the end, not all relationships are uplifting, nurturing, or healing. In all cases, this brokenness effects in one way or another the four basic relationships of our life: with God, with our own selves, with other persons, and with creation.

Exploring our relationships immediately raises basic and serious questions. How do we understand God and relate to Him? Do we see God as a loving Father or a vengeful taskmaster? How do we see ourselves? Do we see ourselves as intrinsically valuable to God and endowed with value and dignity by Him? How do we see others? Do we see other human persons also as valuable and endowed with dignity by the same good and loving God? How do we see the physical world, including our own body? Do we properly appreciate the physical world, including our own body, as a gift and blessing from God?

Healing begins and growth in holiness is renewed as we reestablish and strengthen our true and authentic relationships in the presence of the Living God.

The rich theological tradition of Orthodox Christianity has much insight to offer us in our quest to strengthen authentic relationships and to heal the brokenness resulting from damaged relationships. This does not mean that we can ignore insights gained from the natural and social sciences. Many of these insights can be very helpful. Indeed, many recent studies in psychology and biology confirm the importance of authentic relationships for a meaningful and healthy life. This should come as no surprise to those who are aware of the insights from the great teachers of Eastern Christianity. As Christians, we center our perspectives of life upon the teachings of our Lord Jesus Christ as expressed by His Church through the ages. From the words and deeds of our Lord, we have the divinely given means to deepen our relationships with the Triune God, our true selves, others, and the whole creation.

I believe that we must begin our discussion on relationships by identifying some aspects of our understanding of the Triune God.

Chapter 2

The Holy Trinity: Persons in Relationship

Based upon the reality of the Risen Christ and His teachings, the faith of the Orthodox Church offers profound insights into the mystery of the Triune God and the manner that He relates to us.

God is ultimately a mystery that we cannot fully fathom with our reason alone. Yet, at the same time we affirm that God has revealed something about Himself in order to love us and to draw us closer to Him both in this life and in the life to come. In order to deepen our understanding of all relationships, we must first look at the vision of the Triune God that is central to the faith of Orthodox Christians.

The Mysterious Depth of the Triune God

The Orthodox Christian experience affirms that there is a profound depth to the reality of God who is both unknown and known by us. The events of the Theophany (cf. Mt. 3:13-17; Mk. 1:9-11; Lk. 3:21-22) at the beginning of Christ's ministry and the Transfiguration (cf. Mt. 17:1-8; Mk. 9:2-8; Lk. 9:28-36) at the beginning of His passion vividly bear witness to this mysterious depth of the Triune God. The profound mystery of who God is, of what God is, and of where God is will always elude us. The Existing One is completely other than the creation. As the Orthodox faith has always affirmed, the very essence of God remains unknown to us. There is a mystery to the reality of God which is forever beyond our full understanding. At the same time, the Orthodox Christian faith affirms that God has revealed Himself to us. The living God, who is truly beyond all and who is radically unknowable in His essence, at the same time has willed to be revealed to us in love.

This divine revelation is at once an expression of relationship. The One who is beyond approach has chosen to approach humanity in love for the sake of our salvation. As the psalmist says: "The Lord is God and has revealed himself to us" (Ps. 118.26). These words are said daily in the morning prayers of the Church as a reminder of the centrality of God's revelation.

To affirm the preeminence of divine revelation is also to profess that the way in which God encounters us is not dependent upon our receptivity or understanding. And, the way that we approach the living God is not left to our limited power of human analysis and reflection, which certainly have value. God is not an impersonal force or power whom we seek to know on our own effort. The words of Psalm 118 remind us that our faith, our hope, our love and our prayers are centered in the reality of the living God who has revealed Himself. God has acted, and continues to act in love to communicate with us and to establish a bond with us. Through this divine revelation, we have come to experience and to know the one God as Father, Son and Holy Spirit.

St. Gregory the Theologian speaks of this gradual unfolding of the divine plan of salvation when he says: "The Old Testament openly proclaimed the Father, but proclaimed the Son only dimly. The New Testament manifested the Son but only hinted at the divinity of the Spirit. And now the Spirit lives in our midst, providing us with a clearer demonstration of Himself."[1]

The center of this divine revelation is the coming of our Lord Jesus Christ. He comes to us to embody the Father's love for us. The event of the incarnation of the Son of God establishes a new relationship between God and humanity. All of humanity has been forever affected by His coming. As St. John says: "The Word became flesh and dwelt among us, full of grace and truth: we have beheld His glory, glory as of the only begotten Son of the Father" (Jn. 1:14).

This new relationship is vividly expressed in the ministry of Christ. In His preaching and teachings, Christ reveals to us both the Triune God and the God-centered nature of the human person. Our Lord teaches us about the immanence and intimate closeness of God our Father. We see this in places where Jesus testifies to His relationship with God the Father whom He declares to be our Father as well. He teaches us that no one comes to the Father except through Him (cf. Jn. 6:44-51, 8:12; 14:6). Christ is the Person through whom we find our way to the Father's house (cf. Mt. 10:32-33,40; Mk. 8:38; Lk. 9:26). Throughout His ministry, Christ speaks to us of the loving Father who cares for each of us and awaits our free response in love.

In calling together the first apostles and disciples, Christ establishes the Church in its embryonic form. It is a new people of God who share in a community of faith and love centered upon the divine acts of reconciliation. Within this community of believers, the relationships of persons with the Triune God and with one another are nurtured and strengthened through the presence of the Holy Spirit. They share in the "bond of peace in the unity of the Spirit" (Eph. 4:3).

In His acts of forgiveness, Christ declares God's love for each of His sons and daughters. In His healings and exorcisms, and especially in His own death and Resurrection, Christ proclaims the ultimate victory of God over every force of evil which seeks to break the bond of love between human persons and God. Indeed, at the very heart of Christ's ministry, the Resurrection of the Lord is a bold victory over the power of Satan, sin and death. It is the enduring proclamation that not even death is an ultimate obstacle to the Father's reconciling love.

There is a profound interrelationship between the activity of Christ and the activity of the Spirit as each accomplishes the Father's plan of salvation. The redemptive work of Christ, sent by the Father, cannot be fully appreciated apart from the sanctifying work of the Holy Spirit. Mindful of this, St. Irenaeus of Lyons often spoke poetically of the Son and the Spirit as the "hands" of God. The Son and the Spirit act together to accomplish the will of the Father.[2] Both Son and Spirit work in harmony with each other to fulfill the Father's desire that "all be saved and come to the knowledge of the truth" (1 Tim. 2:4).

Without in any way diminishing the centrality of Christ's saving work on earth, there is a sense that the Lord's activity was also a preparation for the coming of the Holy Spirit. In the mysterious plan of salvation, Christ ascended to the glory of the Father so that the Spirit may come. Indeed, Christ said that "it is to your advantage that I go away, for if I do not go away, the Advocate will not come to you; but if I go, I will send Him to you" (Jn. 16:7). Remembering the Lord's words, St. Symeon the New Theologian says: "The goal of all Christ's actions is the coming of the Holy Spirit."[3] Indeed, it is the Spirit who reveals the presence of the risen Christ in every place and in every age.

Christ does not become an absent Savior after His Ascension. With the coming of the Spirit, it is the Paraclete who mediates the presence and action of Christ. Christ promised that the Spirit will come to us in His name and bear witness to Him and His teachings (cf. Jn. 15:26, Acts 2:33). This is the same Spirit who reminds us of what the Lord has said and who enables us to call God, Father (Jn. 14:25-26, Mt. 6:9). The Spirit does not point to Himself. Rather, the Paraclete always heralds the presence of the Risen Christ in our midst. The Spirit leads us to Christ and permits us to participate in the reign of God in the present. Regardless of how far we are from Palestine in space and time, we know Jesus Christ as Lord today because of the activity of the Holy Spirit (1 Cor. 12:3).

As expressed in the Orthodox tradition, the historic Christian experience of God affirms that the one God is a communion of three divine persons: Father, Son and Holy Spirit who exist in loving relationship with each other. Each is co-eternal. Each is fully God. Yet, each is a distinctive divine person. Each divine person is unique and irreducible to the other, as each enjoys all the same qualities of the other and the fullness of divinity. This is part of the mysterious character of the Triune God.

The Orthodox take very seriously the relationships among the persons of the Divine Trinity. The Son and Spirit are not merely "aspects" or "modes" of God the Father. So much does the Church affirm the unique identities of each divine person within the one God that in the past some have accused believers of teaching polytheism. Such an accusation, however, failed to recognize the distinction of the oneness of God, the divine essence, and the distinction of the three persons. But, historically the explanation of this stance toward the Mystery of the Triune God has been explained by the following mathematical equation: 1+1+1=1.

Speaking specifically about the relationship of the persons of the Trinity, St. Gregory the Theologian says:

> We assert there is nothing lacking, for God has no deficiency. But the difference of manifestation or rather their mutual relations one to another causes the differences of their names. For indeed, it is not some deficiency in the Father which prevents him from being the Son. For the Father is not the Son, and yet this is not due to deficiency or subordination of essence.[4]

The difference among the persons is not one of nature. We profess that Father, Son and Holy Spirit share the one divine nature. Each is fully and perfectly God. Rather, the difference or distinction of persons reflects the manner in which each person relates with the other. The Father is the unbegotten one, the Son is the begotten one and the Spirit is the one who proceeds. The distinguishing characteristic of each is ultimately relational. The persons are fully divine, co-equal, co-eternal. But, each person is distinct in the manner which the one person relates to the others.

There is also an important additional point to be made. While each divine person is distinctive from the other, each is not autonomous or separate from the other. Each person is bound to the others in a relationship of communion. One person cannot be conceived of without making reference to the others. One cannot be separated from the others. Each shares in the reality of the others within the presence of the others. Yes, this is the Mystery of the Triune God.

St. Gregory of Nyssa makes this important affirmation when he says:

> In the life creating nature of the Father, Son and Holy Spirit there is no division but only a continuous and inseparable communion between them. It is not possible to envisage any severance or division, such that one might think of the Son without the Father, or separate the Spirit from the Son. There is between them an ineffable and inconceivable communion and distinction.[5]

The great Church Fathers of the fourth century were especially mindful of the relationship among the three persons of the Trinity. Remembering the scriptural witness and nurtured by prayer, the Fathers affirmed that the divine persons were distinct in their relationships to one another. It was not that one person was superior or that another was inferior. It was not that one person lacked something that another possessed. Each person was fully and completely divine. Yet, each person of the Trinity was in a distinctive relationship with the others.

From outside of time and creation, each person of the Uncreated Trinity abides in the other, in a "dance" (*perichoresis*) of loving surrender. The Triune God exists as persons in authentic relationship. And this relationship is based essentially in loving surrender of one to the other, without confusing the divine persons.

Discussing the relationship among the divine persons, Metropolitan John Zizioulas of Pergamon states:

> *To be* and *to be in relation* become identical. For someone or something *to be*, two things are simultaneously needed: being itself (*hypostasis*) and *being in relation* (i.e., being a person). It is only in relationship that identity appears as having an ontological significance, and if any relationship did not imply such an ontologically meaningful identity, then it would be no relationship.[6]

Fr. Dumitru Staniloae continues this line of thought when he says:

For Christianity, God is a Trinity of persons who have all in common, that is, their entire being, yet are not confused with one another as persons. This implies a perfect love. For love seeks complete unity and reciprocal affirmation of the persons who love one another. Here the absolute is tri-personal, not something impersonal. But the person is assured through the perfect love between one person and the other who have their own basis in the common essence. A person in total solitude cannot be the absolute.[7]

The Loving Outreach of the Triune God

The second affirmation is that this same Triune God reaches out, goes far beyond Himself, and extends Himself in love. While the Living God is forever distinct from the creation, He has willed to reveal Himself within the creation and to share His love in a special way with His human creatures. God seeks to be in a dynamic relationship with us, His most precious creatures! This reaching out in love and for the sake of love can be seen in every act of creation. It was out of love that God chose to create us and the entire cosmos. In addition, God has willed to unite Himself with us in the person of Christ. Likewise, God has willed in love to dwell within each of us through the coming of the Holy Spirit.

This reaching out in love is most powerfully expressed in the event of the incarnation of the Son of God. For our salvation, God has entered into this life in the person of Jesus Christ. It was a profound expression of divine love. It was an act intended to restore humankind and all creation to communion with God the Father. In the words of St. John: "God so loved the world that He sent His Only Begotten Son that whoever believes in Him should not be lost but have eternal life. For God did not send His Son into the world to condemn the world but that the world might be saved through Him"(Jn. 3:16-17).

With the words of a poet, St. Nicholas Cabasilas speaks about this divine love when he says:

> God pours Himself out in an ecstasy of love. He does not remain in the Heavens and call to Himself the servant He loves. No, He Himself descends and searches out for such a servant, and comes near, and lets His love be seen, as He seeks what is like Himself. From those who despise Him, He does not depart; He shows no anger toward those who defy Him, but follows them to their very doors, and endures all things, and even dies, in order to demonstrate His love. All this is true, but we have not yet declared the highest things of all: for not merely does God enter in close fellowship with His servants and extend to them His hand, but He has given Himself wholly to us, so that we become temples of the Living God, and our members are the members of Christ. The head of these members is worshipped by the cherubim, and these hands and feet are joined to that heart.[8]

It is always difficult to find words that can faithfully point to this movement of love. Fr. Staniloae strives to describe this movement of love in the Holy Trinity when he says:

> It is within this supreme unity and love which affirm the eternity of the divine persons that the foundation is laid whereby the interior love of the Trinity can be perceived in the work it directs ad extra. The creation wrought by the Trinity must also be touched by the effects of this unity in diversity.[9]

In other words, there is a dynamic character to the Trinitarian God, as He reaches out to the human person who is the crown of creation. This is affirmed by us in every celebration of the Divine Liturgy. During the anaphora of the Liturgy of St. John Chrysostom, we declare: "From non-existence, you brought us into being, and when we had fallen away you raised us up again. You have never ceased to do everything to lead us into heaven and to bestow upon us your kingdom which is to come..."[10]

God creates out of love not out of necessity. He creates in order to share Himself in a deeply personal manner with another reality. The Father sends the Son, not out of necessity but out of love. He sends the Son in order to restore us to His fellowship. The Word of God willingly accepts a type of divine humiliation in order to bear witness to this love. The Father sends the Spirit not out of necessity but out of love. The Spirit willingly accepts the mission to dwell among us and enable us to respond to the One who first loves us.

We can see the extent of God's love for us in the icon of the Resurrection of Christ which is sometimes called "The Descent into Hades." This is one of the most distinctive and prominent icons in the Orthodox Tradition. The icon presents us with a deeper insight into the historical event of the Resurrection which is the central teaching of the Christian faith and to our identity as believers.

The icon shows the Risen Christ dressed in brilliant white robes. He stands on the broken gates of Hades – the place of the dead. While we can barely see the imprints of the wounds in His hands and His side, this scene does little to remind us of the tragedy of the Crucifixion. Now, He is truly the Victorious Christ standing above the rock of the gates of Hades that looks like a cross. He is truly the Resurrection and the Life (Jn. 11:25)

When we look carefully at the icon, we see that the Risen Christ is not alone. He is reaching out! His hands grasp two others. And, in this depiction of the profound inner meaning of the Resurrection, the Risen Christ is grasping the wrists of a man and a woman. With Christ as their leader and guide, Adam and Eve are being lifted up out of their tomb. Their faces are turned to the Risen Christ with expressions of faith and trust. We also notice that while the Lord firmly grasps their wrists in His hands, they are not being dragged against their will. On the contrary, Adam and Eve, as representatives of all humanity, are freely yielding to the love of God in Christ. The icon seeks to remind us that the Resurrection of Christ is the ultimate victory over the power of alienation, sin, Satan and death. The love of God in Christ has overcome once and for all the evil powers which seek to separate humanity from God. The Resurrection of Christ is also the resurrection of all humanity as symbolized especially by the figures of Adam and Eve.

The Orthodox profess faith in the Triune God who not only has revealed Himself but also has manifested Himself as a good God who is *Philanthropos*, the one who loves humankind.[11] This proclamation of the philanthropic God is at the heart of Orthodox worship, at the heart of Orthodox missions, and at the heart of Orthodox pastoral care in every place and at every time. Over and over in the prayers of the Orthodox Church, we hear the bold affirmation: "You are a good God who loves humankind and to you we offer glory, Father, Son and Holy Spirit…"

The Communal Actions of the Triune God

The third affirmation is that every activity of the Triune God in the work of salvation is a communal action. It is only through the eyes of faith that we distinguish the Father, Son and Holy Spirit in their persons and through their particular activities. They do not, however, act alone. In the process of creation as well as in their loving concern for us and our salvation, Father, Son and Holy Spirit always act in a harmonious interrelationship.

And during His ministry, Jesus points to the common activity of the persons of the Trinity on a number of occasions. He affirms repeatedly that He came to do the will of the Father. In the Gospel of John, for example, the Lord says, "whoever believes in Me believes not only in Me but also in the one who sent Me, and whoever sees Me sees the one who sent Me" (Jn. 12:44-45). Later in this same gospel, we read the account of His discourse during the Last Supper where He says to the disciples: "Do you not believe that I am in the Father and the Father in me? The words that I speak to you I do not speak on my own. The Father who dwells in me is doing His works. Believe me that I am in the Father and the Father is in me..." (Jn. 14:10-11). And later, the Lord declares that the Father will send the Spirit through Him (Jn. 14:15-17, 15: 26-27).

St. Gregory the Theologian affirms the interrelationship of the divine persons when he says:

> No sooner do I conceive the one that I am illuminated by the splendor of the three. No sooner do I distinguish them that I am carried back to the one. When I think of any one of the three, I think of the one as a whole and my eyes are filled, and the greater part of what I am thinking escapes me.[12]

The actions of the Father, Son and Holy Spirit do not separate one from the other. They share a common divine essence and, therefore, they are united in their activity. The action of one person mysteriously points to the others. There is a reciprocal relationship among the divine persons. The persons act in concert with each other. St. Gregory of Nyssa says:

> We do not learn that the Father does something on His own in which the Son does not cooperate. Or rather that the Son acts on His own without the Spirit. Rather, every operation which extends from God to creation is described according to our differing conception of it, has its origin in the Father, proceeds through the Son and reaches completion by the Holy Spirit.... For the action of each in any matter is not separate and individualized. But whatever occurs ... takes place through the three persons, and is not a separate thing.[13]

There is a complementary and reciprocal relationship among the three persons of the Trinity. As with the acts of creation, the acts of redemption and sanctification also involve each person of the Holy Trinity.

The icon of the Hospitality of Abraham and Sarah is a valuable visual expression of the interrelationship of the persons of the Trinity. The icon depicts the visitation of God to Abraham and Sarah by the oak of Mamre. According to the story (Genesis 18), three men came to the home of Abraham and Sarah. The visitors express the presence of the Triune God to Abraham and Sarah who freely offer loving hospitality to the strangers. The icon of this dramatic visitation of God does not depict visually the persons of the Trinity. Rather, the mysterious three visitors are shown in the icon as winged angels in order to express the presence of the persons of the Trinity. The icon presents the three angels seated at table. They appear the same and yet each has distinguishing characteristics. They look to one another, as if expressing a loving and humble relationship to each other. The image of the three angels is meant to direct us to the persons of the Trinity and their intimate relationship. At the same time, the encounter between the mysterious visitors and Abraham and Sarah expresses the relationship between the Triune God and humanity. It is a relationship of love and intimacy.

The goal of God's saving activity is the salvation of humanity and the world. It is true that only the Son of God became incarnate for us and our salvation. The Father did not become incarnate, nor did the Holy Spirit. But this wondrous act of divine love took place by the power of the Holy Spirit and in order to fulfill the will of the Father who desires that all be saved and come to the knowledge of the truth (I Tim. 2:4). St. Irenaeus of Lyons expresses the intimate relationship between the persons of the Trinity when he says: "In the name of Christ is implied the anointed, the anointer, and the unction. The Father is the anointer, the Son is the Anointed and the Holy Spirit is the unction."[14]

When we come to recognize the relationship which the Triune God offers to us, we are led to a sense of gratitude and thanksgiving for all the blessings which we have received. With the words of David the Psalmist, we too can raise our voices and joyously declare:

> Bless the Lord, O my soul.
> From the depth of my being,
> Bless His holy name.
> Bless the Lord, O my soul,
> Forget not all His favors.
> He it is who pardons all your failings,
> Who cures all your ills,
> Who preserves your life from deadly peril,
> Who crowns you with tenderness and mercy,
> Who fills your lifetime with goodness,
> Who restores your youth like the eagle's. (Psalm 103:1-5)

The dramatic and loving actions of the Triune God are always far more than we could hope for or expect. God never gives up on us! While we may forget His gracious actions, He never abandons us. He always cares for us as His precious daughters and sons. He constantly seeks us, and calls us to return to the household of love, peace, and healing.

This brief discussion certainly does not exhaust every aspect of the relationship between the Father, Son and Holy Spirit. However, these affirmations provide us with a theological foundation to assert that from an Orthodox perspective the ultimate reality is based upon the one God who exists as three persons. The Father, Son and Holy Spirit are bound together in an intimate relationship of love. The relationship among the persons of the Trinity is meant to be reflected in our human relationships. As many Orthodox theologians have consistently repeated: The Trinitarian God is the ultimate paradigm of human relations. The manner in which we view ourselves, the way we relate to one another as Christians and the manner by which we structure our Church are meant to reflect the reality of God. Known throughout the Gospel of Christ, the Holy Trinity is our ultimate example and model.

Notes

[1] St. Gregory the Theologian, *Oration* 31.1.26

[2] St. Irenaeus, *Against Heresies*, 4: preface; 4:10, 1; 5:1,3

[3] St. Symeon the New Theologian, *Homil*, 38.

[4] St. Gregory the Theologian, *Fifth Theological Oration*, 9.

[5] St. Gregory of Nyssa, *On the Difference between Essence and Hypostasis*, 4. (Identified at Chalcedon as St. Basil's Letter 38).

[6] John Zizioulas, *Being as Communion*, (Crestwood, NY: St. Vladimir's Seminary Press, 1985), 88.

[7] Dumitru Staniloe, *The Experience of God*, Ioan Ionita and Robert Barringer, trans., (Brookline, MA: Holy Cross Orthodox Press, 1994), 68.

[8] St. Nicholas Cabasilas, *On the Divine Liturgy*, 2:132.

[9] Ibid., 68.

[10] The Liturgy of St. John Chrysostom

[11] See, Metropolitan Maximos Aghiorgoussis, *In the Image of God* (Brookline: Holy Cross Orthodox Press, 1999), 114-125.

[12] St. Gregory the Theologian, *Orations on Holy Baptism*, 40:41.

[13] St. Gregory of Nyssa, "An Answer to Ablabios: That We Should Not Think of Saying that There Are Three Gods."

[14] St. Irenaeus of Lyons, *Against Heresies*, 3:18

Chapter 3

The Human Person in Relationship: Some Corollary Affirmations

We noted in the previous chapter that the Orthodox Christian faith makes a number of important and foundational affirmations about the Triune God. These affirmations are rooted in the Gospel of Christ and are, therefore, essential to our understanding of reality. We affirm the mysterious depth of the Triune God. We affirm that God, the Philanthropos, reaches out in love. And, we affirm that the actions of the Triune God are communal. Mindful of these affirmations about the Triune God, we can also make a number of corollary affirmations about the human person. These affirmations are also rooted in Christ and His Gospel as taught by the Church through the centuries.

The Mystery of the Human Person

We believe that every human person is created by God and is by nature theocentric. Each of us is a psycho-somatic person who is related to the Triune God in the very depth of our being. From the very moment of our creation by the One who loves us, the human person is fashioned with an orientation to the source of life and holiness. This inner orientation to the divine is at the very center of our identity. It is the utmost reality of our existence regardless of whether we recognize it or not.

The Theocentric Person

There is a natural and enduring relationship between each human person and the Triune God. It is a relationship which can never be destroyed although it can be distorted by our sins. This relationship is rooted in the very act of divine creation. God is both our Creator and our Father. We are always His daughters and sons because of our inherent relationship with Him. We are valuable because God the Father treasures us as His own.

This special relationship is deepened through the coming of Christ who has united Himself fully with our humanity. The followers of Christ believe that He has become one with us in order to reveal our true identity and value. He is "the way, the truth and the life" (Jn. 14:6). This essential identity that Christ revealed is manifested to the believer through the activity of the Holy Spirit in the life of the Church. We know God because of His continued self-disclosure. Likewise, as Christians, we know the deepest identity of the human person because of this divine revelation.

It is normal and natural for human persons to be in relationship with God because He has established this connection in the very act of creation. The human person is truly "Theocentric." A natural and loving relationship with God is fundamental to human identity. Reflecting this tradition, St Basil the Great makes this point when he says:

> The love of God is not taught. No one has taught us to enjoy the light or to be attached to life more than anything else. And no one has taught us to love the two people who brought us into the world. Which is all the more reason to believe that we did not learn to love God as a result of outside instruction. In the very nature of the human person has been sown the ability to love. You and I ought to welcome this seed, cultivate it carefully, nourish it attentively and foster its growth by going to the school of God's commandments.
>
> You and I have received from God the natural tendency to follow His commandments ... God would not have given us the commandment to love Him without also giving us the natural faculty for loving Him.[1]

This is a remarkable and very powerful observation. Like the Eastern Fathers generally, St. Basil affirms a relational orientation between Creator and creature that God Himself has established in the very structure of our being. He tells us that we have an innate power of loving God from the moment of our creation. This loving orientation is essential to our human identity. The seed was planted in us by God from our very beginning. St. Basil also affirms that both nurture and direction is needed for this love to grow. This inner and divinely given orientation is like a spark, he says, which needs to be kindled. It is an expression of love that needs to be carefully cultivated and skillfully nurtured. Based on his understanding of God's creative activity, Basil is very clear that the genesis of this love is God Himself. God the Holy Trinity first acts in the lives of each of us. And, because of this, we are by nature desirous of the beautiful. And, that which is truly beautiful is the good. And that which is truly good, is God!

St. Basil affirms that we have an innate longing to love God, and to know God as the source of life. This knowledge is not necessarily "of the mind" but rather it is, first of all, "of the heart." The "heart" in this case, does not merely refer to the sentimental seat of the emotions. Instead, "heart" refers to the center of the human person. It is the seat, so to speak, where our deepest intentions, values and priorities abide. The "heart" is where we each choose to respond to divine Truth, in particular, even as we are usually not aware of this.[2] This perspective reminds us of our Lord's statement: "For where your treasure is, there will your heart be also. (Mt. 6:21)"

The Dignity of Each Person

Every human person has profound value and dignity precisely because of the essential and profound relationship with the Triune God. The Book of Genesis expresses this conviction by affirming that we are created in the "image and likeness" of God (Gen. 1:26, 5:1). No other aspect of the creation is described in this way in the marvelous story of Creation. The words express the special character of the human person who is part of Creation, but also distinct from the rest of created reality. This important affirmation is also made in the New Testament where humanity is regarded as a creation of God (Acts 17:28) as well as fashioned in God's image and likeness (Col. 3:10, Jas. 3:9).

The stories of our Lord in the Gospels convey this profound perspective on the identity and value of the human person. Christ encountered many people during the course of His ministry. Some of these encounters have been recorded for our benefit by the Evangelists. They show us that our Lord came into contact with many types of people: men and women, Jews and Gentiles, believers and non-believers, wealthy and poor, healthy and ill, outcasts and insiders. We could recall Christ's encounter with Zacchaeus the tax collector (Lk. 19:2f), or the Samaritan woman at the well whom the Church has named Photini (Jn. 4:7f). We could also think of the Roman centurion (Matt. 8:5f), the woman caught in adultery (Jn.8: 3f), or Bartimaeus the blind beggar (Mk. 10:46f).

In every one of these encounters and in many others, Jesus has honored the person before Him. Our Lord respected the mystery of each person who was created by God, and therefore His treasured daughter or son. He respected each person regardless of gender, race, physical condition, religious convictions or status in society. Even if they had sinned, He valued them even in spite of their sin. Our Lord may not have always approved of the behavior of the persons He met. Yet, He saw every person as a child of God and treated them with dignity. Because of this, Jesus transcended the customs and mores of His day.

Jesus was accused of violating the scriptural prohibitions and breaking religious laws of the Jewish people of His day. The dignity and value of the person was not always recognized by others around Him. Indeed, there were those who treated sinners, women, the sick, the disabled and foreigners as greatly inferior in value as compared to themselves. These people were treated with contempt especially by those who claimed to uphold the religious laws of the day. Contrary to this, our Lord loved each person and treated each person with profound respect.

Based upon the teachings and ministry of Christ, the Fathers and great Teachers of the Church have affirmed the belief that each person is created in the "image and likeness" of God. This affirmation certainly does not mean that we resemble God in a physical sense. Rather, it means that God has both created us and has endowed us with a special relationship with Him. Our deepest identity as a human person is given to us by God. Our deepest value as a human person is affirmed by God.

St. Gregory of Nyssa says to us:

> You do have within your grasp the degree of knowledge of God which you can attain. For, when God made you, He at once endowed your nature with this perfection: upon the structure of your nature He imprinted an imitation of the perfection of His own nature, just as one would impress upon wax the outline of an emblem… You must then wash away, by a life of virtue, the dirt that clings to your heart like plaster, and then your divine beauty will once again shine forth.[3]

Our value as a human person, therefore, is not determined by our accomplishments or lack thereof. Our value is not determined by our age, race, gender, nationality or economic status. Our value is not determined by our mental or physical abilities or disabilities. Indeed, it is not determined by our faith or our religious activities. In spite of all, even our sins, we forever remain daughters and sons of the Heavenly Father, who calls us to live in communion with Him. The person of Christ is for all the model and example of life lived in communion with the Father.[4]

St. Macarius of Egypt powerfully calls attention to our dignity which we enjoy as the sons and daughters of God, when he says:

> Look how mighty are the heavens and the earth, the sun and the moon. But it was not in these that the Lord rested. The human person, therefore, is of more value than all creatures, and I dare say he is more valuable than any creature, visible

> or invisible, more valuable than the ministering angels. When God said: 'Let us make man in our image and after our likeness,' He was not speaking of the Archangels Michael and Gabriel. He was speaking about the spiritual substance of the human person, His immortal soul.[5]

With this remarkable teaching, St. Macarius affirms our dignity and honor that are rooted in God and His love. God has first loved us. God has first honored us. Our challenge is to recognize this truth and to live our lives accordingly.

The unique quality of our personhood begins at the moment of our conception. But, it certainly does not end there. From that time, each person is profoundly affected by his or her particular relationship with God, others and the natural world. Each of us is called to cultivate and deepen our identity. Persons mature in relationship to the reality of life in which they live and grow. This fact points to the distinctive and truly mysterious character of every human person. There is a depth and breadth to every human life that makes it a true mystery. It is mysterious in the sense that each life reflects distinctive encounters and personal choices.

The Fathers of the Church point to the phrase "after our likeness" as a reminder that the human person is called to mature in his or her identity. Every human person is called to grow and deepen their relationship with God, their true self, others and the creation. Authentic relations are meant to mature. In a real sense, we are called to become the persons we were created to be through our relationships of love with God and others! Origen of Alexandria, an early Christian teacher, says that the human race received the dignity of God's image at the beginning of its creation, whereas the perfection is reserved for the end. Human persons must achieve it by imitating God in His works. The possibility of perfection is right there at the beginning by virtue of the image. In the end, human persons will reach perfect likeness by means of their works."[6]

In our day, Archbishop Anastasios of Albania makes the same

affirmation when he says: "Likeness to God is offered to human beings as a possibility, not as an accomplished fact. It is ultimately achieved through the actions of the Holy Spirit."[7] We are not meant to be static. We are called to cultivate our love and to grow in holiness.

God has established a profound bond of love with each human person. This means that it is natural and healthy for the human person to live freely in communion with God. It is unnatural, through the exercise of our free will, for the human person not to be in a loving relationship with God. Such a lack of communion with the source of life is truly a disorientation which shakes the identity of the person and damages all other relationships.

The Gift of Freedom

Each person must strive truly to be a person who lives in communion with God. If we are truly God-centered then each of us has an obligation to live our life in accordance with this orientation. It is in this way that we become the person that God calls us to be. Our true self is expressed when we live in communion with the source of life and holiness.

With this in mind, the Fathers of the Christian East place a special emphasis upon the gift of freedom. The human person is gifted by God with freedom. The freedom to choose is one of our essential human characteristics. St. Gregory the Theologian tells us: "From the beginning, the Creator granted human persons their freedom and a free will. They were bound only by the laws of the commandments."[8]

The freedom that is given to us by God is the basis of our ability to make choices. We have the ability to choose either to grow in our relationship with God or to choose a path of self-centeredness and isolation. This positive choice for God is ultimately an expression of love. God does not force Himself upon us. As a loving Father, He always waits for our free and loving response to His presence and His love.

Speaking of the relationship of virtuous living and freedom of choice, St. John Chrysostom says:

> Since God loves human persons and is benevolent, He does what He can so that we may radiate virtue. God wants us to win glory, and because of this, He does not draw anyone by force or constraint. Rather, God attracts by persuasion and kindness all those who are willing to respond, and so wins them over. Some, therefore received Him when He came, while others did not. God wishes to have no servant who is unwilling or who is forced into service. God wants all to come of their own free will and choice, and with gratitude to Him for this grace.[9]

While discussing the Orthodox understanding of person, Ecumenical Patriarch Bartholomew of Constantinople takes care to stress the importance of freedom. He says,

> The human being, as an existential reality, can be a person only when living in freedom. Only in conditions in which the full range of possibilities is open to our free and conscious choice are we able to transform our temporal reality and ourselves into the image of the divine kingdom. Our humanity is realized through the free act of relationship with others. Personhood is a free act of communion that makes heterogeneity and uniqueness fundamental aspects of our humanity.[10]

The most important choice that a person can make is the decision to relate with God by responding freely in love to His love. In this sense, true human freedom is first and foremost expressed through communion with God. When persons do not choose to live in communion with God, they are not truly free. They easily become attracted to and enslaved by idols. This free decision to live in communion with God is fundamental to every other relationship.

The Example of Mary

The Orthodox have always found the willingness of Mary the Theotokos to share in the work of salvation as a powerful expression of human freedom. The story of the Annunciation is found in the Gospel of Luke (1: 26-56). When the angel relates God's plan to Mary, he shares God's hope for the entire cosmos. God took a risk of infinite proportions at that moment since Mary, on behalf of all humanity, could have said "No." The angel has to wait for her response. And, it is with both wonder and humility that Mary joyfully offers her consent and, by so doing, speaks on behalf of every man and woman who seek to have God enter their life.

Mary said "yes" to the divine invitation and becomes a "new Eve." Her free and intentional act of obedience is in contrast to the willful disobedience we see in the story of Adam and Eve. The "old Eve" refused to cooperate with the will of God for her life. She and Adam chose to turn away from God in order to become gods without God. This alienated them from God's life-giving providence and, consequently, from each other. Their action seems to set a pattern for subsequent generations. From this point on, human relationships became distorted. Human persons passed on from one generation to the next the propensity for distorted relationships which further misdirected them from authentic life with God, one another, and creation.

With Mary's "yes" to the angelic invitation to participate in God's plan of salvation, she has become a model for every person who wishes freely to respond to God's invitation. Because of her free response, the Fathers of the Church viewed Mary as the "new Eve." This important theme can be found in the writings of early Christians.

St. Irenaeus reflects the tradition when he says:

> Just as Eve, wife of Adam, yes, yet still a virgin became by her disobedience the cause of death for herself and for the whole human race, so Mary, too, betrothed but still a virgin, became through her obedience the cause of salvation for herself

> and the whole human race…and so it was that the knot of Eve's disobedience was loosed by Mary's obedience. For what the virgin Eve bound fast by her refusal to believe, the Virgin Mary unbound by her faith.[11]

Mary intentionally and without coercion exercised her freedom by responding in love to the Father's invitation to bear the Son of God. While the manifestation of her vocation was certainly distinctive, Mary expressed the freedom to love and to serve God. Such is the calling of every human person.

Freedom To Choose the Good

There are two additional aspects of the gift of freedom that should be noted. The first is the recognition of our freedom to choose the good and not to sin. Sin is a topic that is frequently denied and avoided in many circles today. From an Orthodox perspective, sin is not defined so much in terms of abstract, yet judgmental, moralistic rules from which one can waver. On a deeper level, sin is viewed as a deviation from the good. This deviation is personal. It is an expression of personal choice. Some have described sin as "missing the mark." Yet, the decision to sin has profound consequences not only for ourselves but also for our relationships. The decision to sin effects negatively our relationship with our own selves, with others, with creation and God. When we look at how fractured the Christian community and the broader society can become, we would do well to acknowledge that these divisions are the consequences of human sin.

We were not created by our heavenly Father to sin but to share in His goodness and life. Therefore, sin is profoundly unnatural! Sin is a distortion of living that is especially beneath the dignity of those who are called to follow Christ. Sin can be avoided by living in communion with God and by honoring the dignity of ourselves and others.

Yes, the gift of freedom can be abused. The story of the fall in the Book of Genesis points to the tragic consequences of the abuse of freedom. When Adam and Eve chose to disobey the commandment of God, they sinned. Their action expressed a self-centered desire to live apart from God, to live autonomous existences. Unfortunately, their sin – their abuse of freedom – has consequences that effected their relationship not only with God but also with each other and the whole creation. The story points to the danger of seeking to live apart from God. As such, it is a story that has a profound significance for everyone.

In the New Testament, the Parable of the Prodigal Son has a similar theme (Luke 15:11f). The younger son chooses to run away from home and squanders his inheritance on loose living. He falls into a state of existence where his true identity is distorted. When he finally "comes to his senses," the younger son recognizes his sin and freely returns to his father's house. As the story shows, the father always loved him and never gave up on him. As the son reaches the house, the father runs out to greet him. Despite his claims of unworthiness, the younger son was welcomed home a "son."

Here, it is important to remember what the Fathers of the Church always recognize about the danger of sin and its tragic consequences. Sin is to be avoided. They warn that sin can do great damage to ourselves and to others. Sin can distort our identity and can harm others as well. As St. Gregory of Nyssa says, sin creates "an ugly mask over the beauty of the image."[12]

Yet, at the same time, the Fathers affirm that our dignity remains in spite of the sin. The ugly mask of sin does not destroy the beauty of the image. "No matter how deep the alienation and fall," says Archbishop Anastasios, "human nature never ceases to bear God's image and is therefore in essence good."[13] With God's love, we can always turn from sin and live in accordance with our deepest identity. Like the father in the story of the prodigal son, God treats us as daughters and sons, and waits for us to come to our senses. This is the deepest meaning of repentance. It is a change of heart which leads to reorientation and redirection of our life towards what is good and holy. When this repentance takes place, all our relationships are effected for the better. Repentance means taking away the mask of false living in selfishness and self-centeredness. Repentance means that we return to God as His daughters and sons.

Archbishop Anastasios says that the

> misadventure of the human race is linked to the fact that human beings were endowed with freedom as an essential attribute. They were free to reject unselfish love, which they did, only to become imprisoned in their own egotistical self-love. Nevertheless, despite this self imposed exile, they still possess the identity and heritage of their divine origin, as well as their longing for paradise lost.[14]

Freedom To Grow in Holiness

The second point that must be affirmed is that we have the freedom to grow in holiness. In other words, we are encouraged to respond to the Lord's call to live a new life as His follower. Christ spoke of this when He says: "I have come that they may have life, life in abundance" (Jn. 10:10). Our Lord invites us to move from the dead-end of self-centeredness to God-centeredness, from brokenness to wholeness, from isolation to integration, from sinfulness to fruitfulness. This journey requires time, our best attention, effort and courage. The invitation is truly a gift. It is the basic element in salvation. God is the one who saves! Yet, we must freely and consciously respond to the gift of salvation. So, St Paul tells us to "live a life worthy of the calling to which you have been called, in all lowliness and meekness, with patience, forbearing one another in love, eager to maintain the unity of the Spirit in the bond of peace" (Eph. 4:1-3).

The Orthodox have referred to this process as deification or *theosis*. It is a process in which we grow in holiness through our relationship with the One who is truly holy. It is the process by which we deepen our relationship with the Triune God together with the other relationships, responsibilities and obligations in this life. For the Orthodox, this is the reality of salvation. God the Father has established a new relationship with us in the person of Christ and through His saving activity. This restored relationship is a gift of love offered to us by Christ. Yet, this gift must become real in the lives of each of us through the gift of the Spirit. We must do our part to receive this gift of relationship and to make it our own. Salvation is a process of growth in God within the context of our relationships and responsibilities.

We do not "earn" salvation through our activities or deeds. On the contrary, we receive the gift of salvation and strive to make it our own on a daily basis. Our acts of charity, our prayer, our preparation for and our participation in the Eucharist and our reception of Holy Communion enable us to make the gift of salvation truly our own. The process of salvation is a journey through which we draw closer to God and become the persons He wishes us to be. Like any genuine relationship, our relationship with God requires our own active participation.

Within this journey of faithful discipleship, the believer enters more deeply into the new life offered by God. It is a new life through which the disciple becomes aware of the love of the Father, by means of the saving activity of Christ, through the fellowship of the Holy Spirit. It is a new life where the love of God is shared in a personal way. It is experienced to the very depths of our being. Because of this, God no longer is a distant figure. God is not an abstract concept or an idea which can be debated. God is a loving Person.

For the believer, God is known as our Father, as our ultimate Advocate, and as our gentle and beloved Friend who loves us, and whose goodness elicits our love in return. God is deeply personal. In the words of St. Nicholas Cabasilas, the disciple comes to know God "as more kind than any friend, more just than any ruler, more affectionate than any father, more a part of us than our own limbs, and more necessary to us than our own heart."[15]

In my practice, when people share their concerns with me, I find that at some point in our work together, freedom becomes an important focus of our attention. This is because our capacity to choose freely is at the foundation of every relationship. In contemporary society, whenever we first think of "freedom," we often think of it in terms of "freedom to choose." Freedom is a fundamental aspect of human persons endowed with self-consciousness and a conscience. It is perhaps the most important gift given to each of us by God as this sets us apart from other living creatures.

We become more fully alive and more fully human through the process of freely making choices. To be alive is to choose, and we have the freedom to choose either good or evil at each point in our life. As followers of the Lord, we are called to make choices that reflect our true humanity lived in the presence of God. We are called to make choices that give glory to the Living God. Every day God says to each of us: "I have set before you life and death, blessing and cursing; therefore choose life, that you and your descendants may live, by loving the Lord, your God, heeding His voice, and holding fast to Him. For that will mean life for you." (Deut. 30:19-20.) We are called to choose life!

Our choices also effect others. Each of us is intimately related to others. We are part of a matrix of relationships. The choices that we make do not simply affect our lives. To believe this would be to delude ourselves. True, we may choose to live in an isolated, self-centered manner. Yet, even this choice has an influence upon other persons whether we see it or not. Because we are naturally part of the web of human relationships, our choices have an impact upon the lives of others.

In his 1994 Encyclical Letter commemorating the first day of the new liturgical year (September 1), Ecumenical Patriarch Bartholomew elaborated on this very concern: He stated:

> Scripture informs us that if one member of the body is infirm, the entire body is affected (I Cor. 12:26). There is, after all, solidarity in the human race because, made as they are in the image of the Triune God, human beings are independent and co-inherent. "No man is an island." We are "members of one another" (Eph. 4:25). Therefore, any action, performed by any member of the human race, inevitably affects all others members.

> Consequently, no one falls alone and no one is saved alone. According to Dostoevsky's Staretz Zossima in *The Brothers Karamazov*, we are each of us responsible for everyone and everything.[16]

As a conscious being, the human person is never coerced by the good and loving God to love Him or others. God could have created human beings to be more "automatic," not unlike like engines, robots or computers. This, however, would also negate other important qualities of human personhood that are related to our ability to choose. A robot, for example, cannot love and cannot experience communion with God.

Bishop Kallistos Ware emphasized the importance of the gift of human freedom when he said:

> In a world that grows increasingly dehumanized … there is an urgent need for Christians to insist upon the supreme value of freedom. In the entire universe nothing is more decisive than the deliberate acts of choice made by persons endowed with reason and conscience. As human beings, we are conditioned by our environment and our unconscious motives, but never helplessly enslaved by these things. God has set each of us upon the earth … entrusted with "dominion over every living thing" (Gen. 1:28). Let us not, out of cowardice or lack of imagination, abdicate from this our royal authority.[17]

Essential Qualities For the True Self

St. Irenaeus of Lyons tells us that "The glory of God is a person fully alive and that the vision of God is the life of the human person."[18] These words of Irenaeus point to the fact that God is honored when we are living in a full and authentic manner. At the same time, he reminds us that a life lived in communion with God is meant to be the center of our identity.

Each of us must truly cultivate an honest relationship with our own deepest and truest self. This may sound strange at first, but the point is, that we must strive to live a life with genuine integrity in the presence of the loving God who created us. We do not want to live with a mask that covers and distorts our deepest identity as God's daughters and sons. Therefore, an authentic life in Christ is marked by coherence between our deepest identity as a child of God and the manner in which we live our life. Such a life is marked by continuity between our beliefs and our actions, between our words and our deeds. Such a life is marked by continuous honesty with our own self before God and others. Such a life is marked by integrity before God and others.

St. Paul spoke about the meaning of the genuine human life in terms of the fruits of the Spirit. The person who is truly living a life in Christ, that is to say an honest, faithful, and genuine human life, is the person who manifests the fruits of the Spirit. He says the fruits are "love, joy, peace, patience, kindness, goodness, faithfulness, gentleness, and self-control... If we live by the Spirit, let us also walk by the Spirit. Let us have no self-conceit, no provoking of one another, no envy of one another" (Gal. 5:22-26).

Our call to relate authentically with ourselves, God, others and creation is at the foundation of how we are to live our lives every moment of every day. This approach is challenging, positive and life-giving. At the same time, this kind of radical relational honesty demands humility. Humility is arguably the most powerful virtue in assisting us to become our true selves in the presence of God. Genuine humility requires courage, and in many ways wielding it is counter-intuitive for most of us.

Rather than calling attention to our "personal special-ness" or our "terminal uniqueness," as I often like to call it, we need to consider a different approach. True humility directs us to accept our being "of the earth." We are nothing but dust, created out of the clay of the earth solely for the pleasure and love of God. This is the profound paradox. We are "virtual nothings" who are also "created in the image and after the likeness of God." Our achieving humility is a gift as this indicates that we are deeply grounded in the reality of who we are.

Humility is often confused with humiliation. These two phenomena, however, are very different from each other. Humility signifies our being "right-sized" in the presence of God, and in relationship with other persons and the entire creation. We are not "too big" in the sense of overestimating ourselves. Likewise, we are not "too small" in diminishing our true dignity. True humility recognizes our inherent dignity as a daughter or son of God. It also recognizes that we are not created to be self-sufficient, self-centered individuals! The virtue of humility is an essential characteristic of persons living in authentic relationships.

Some Christians honestly may confuse humility with a self-criticism that may more correctly be identified as humiliation. They may defend this perspective by reminding us that the witness of the saints indicate that the closer one grows to God, the more he or she becomes aware of their sinfulness and finiteness. This is true. This type of profound self-awareness, however, actually reflects a healthy and mature humility. This is because, the saints, through the support of the Lord's own tender merciful assistance, still find the courage to face themselves and to approach Him with faith, hope and love. It is in humility that they both recognize their dignity in the Lord's light and their weakness in His mercy.

Humiliation is also very different from humility. Humiliation is a dangerous and poisonous mechanism used by one human being seeking to diminish and distort the value of other persons. Humiliation is typically used as a weapon to control others. It is all too often, a tool in the merciless service of pride. And so, it is toxic and life-effacing. Humiliation does not enhance the life of another person. The objective of humiliation as a weapon is very precise. The action of humiliation seeks to control and ultimately annihilate the other experientially "from the inside out." This occurs as the person targeted by this abuse is blocked from discerning his or her true value and vocation in the presence of God. Instead, the person may easily fall into the trap of believing that he or she is intrinsically worthless due to the attack of the abuser. This life-effacing dynamic has absolutely nothing to do with the living God of love! Rather, this life-effacing dynamic exemplifies profound spiritual illness.

There are times when the abyss of humiliation is so deep that it tends to create an experience of internal, overwhelming chaos and desperation in the life of the person. This experience may become so overwhelming that the person may be led to believe he or she has no reason to live! Some have called the effects of humiliation, "soul murder."

Humility and humiliation are often confused in the minds and hearts of many persons. This includes persons in leadership, even religious leadership. While we are all called to be persons of humility, no one has the right to humiliate another. There is no justification for such actions or words.

The virtue of humility helps to provide us with the audacity to approach God as His daughters and sons. As creatures bearing the "image and likeness" of God, we are endowed with many gifts founded in our ability to be self-aware and in our free will. While "all have sinned and fall short of the glory of God" (Rm. 3:23), we can still, through the gracious presence of the Holy Spirit, grow in our vocation for authentic relationship with God, others, creation and our own selves.

Sometimes it is difficult to discern if a relationship is authentic or not. Sometimes, this takes time. We are advised to "test the spirits" (1 John 4:1) being mindful of the fruits they produce. In the Gospel of Matthew, Our Lord says to His disciples, "by their fruits you shall know them" (Mt. 7:20).

Through my limited experience, I have come to learn that persons who relate authentically with God, others, creation and themselves are humble persons. This is because they are rooted in reality. They demonstrate the honesty to recognize, the courage to surrender to and the gratitude to receive the love of the living God. While we may not see this through their daily, mundane activities, their stance in life, so to speak, is reflected by the orans position. This is the prayer stance of the early church, where the faithful believer stands to meet the Lord in the Holy Spirit with head erect, eyes open, ears attentive and hands empty, raised in loving self-offering surrender and prayer.

Not unlike the wise virgins in the parable told by our Lord

(Mt. 25:1-13), humble persons are courageous and receptive persons. At the cost of looking foolish to the other truly "foolish" maidens, the wise women prepared themselves as fully as possible. They "took flasks of oil with their lamps" (v. 4). They anticipated the enormity of the surrounding darkness and the potential long wait. They focused their attention on the arrival of their Beloved Bridegroom doing what they could to prepare to meet Him. This highly disciplined and mindful effort, *askesis*, is completely dependent upon continuous, personal, unconditional honesty in the presence of God; first with God and themselves, then with others and creation. As this is a living relationship, humble people avoid "falling asleep." They examine themselves in the presence of God. St. Gregory of Nyssa speaks of the importance of truly knowing ourselves when he says:

> Our greatest protection is self-knowledge and the avoidance of the delusion that we are seeing ourselves when we are really looking at something else. This is what happens to those who do not examine themselves: What they see is strength, beauty, reputation, political power, great wealth, pomp, self-importance, bodily stature…and they think that this is what they really are. Such persons make very poor guardians of themselves. Because of their absorption in something else, they overlook what is their own and leave it unguarded. How can a person protect what he does not know? The most secure protection for our treasure is to know ourselves: each one of us must know himself as he is so that he may not be unconsciously protecting something else other than himself.

"Know yourself," says Bishop Kallistos Ware,

> means 'know yourself as God-sourced, God-shaped', acknowledge your divine origin, rec-

ognize that you are a sacred being. Apart from God, we are unintelligible as human persons. The divine is the determining element in our humanness; losing our sense of the divine, we lose also our sense of the human.[20]

Love Beyond Self

The human person is called to express a love which reaches beyond self – to God, to others and, ultimately, to the entire creation. In our discussion of the persons of the Holy Trinity, we noted that each divine person is open to the other. God is a Trinity of divine persons who abide in each other in an eternal "dance," *perichoresis* in Greek, of mutual loving surrender. Each is in a loving relationship with the other. This Trinitarian love, however, is not a closed circuit. But rather, it overflows towards the entire creation and especially towards each and every person.

We, too, in our own distinctively human way, are called to this same vocation for authentic relationships. We, too, are called to reach out in love, to grow in communion with God and each other in ways that express this joyful "dance" of loving surrender. We human persons, created in the divine "image and likeness" (Gen. 1:26), are called to do exactly the same on a creaturely level.

The supreme example for us is always the loving surrender of the Son of God who freely entered into our midst in Christ for us and for our salvation. The ancient adage of St. Athanasius declares: "God became a human person so that the human person may become divine."[21] This affirmation about God and His overflowing love points to our vocation. As God, so to say, "went beyond Himself" for our salvation, so also we are called to reach beyond ourselves to the Other, to others and to the entire creation.

Jesus emphasizes this truth in the Gospels every time He speaks about the importance of love. One day, He was asked directly which commandment was the greatest. The Lord responded: "You shall love the Lord your God with all your heart, and with all your soul, and with all your mind; this is the first and great commandment. And the second is like it, you shall love your neighbor as yourself" (Mt. 22:37-39). According to these words, the Lord teaches that His follower is one who loves God, and others and self. These three expressions of love are intimately related. Love in its various expressions is the basis of every authentic relationship.

The Ministry of Reconciliation

Those who enjoy a mature relationship with God are a therapeutic presence to others. Consciously and often unconsciously, we can become vehicles for the healing presence of God in the many situations in which we find ourselves. We cannot simply be followers of Christ. We can also be signs and expressions of Christ's presence. Through our relationships with others, we can help other persons grow in authentic relationship with themselves, others, creation and God.

Yes, we are called to join with the Triune God in a ministry of reconciliation and healing in this world. We are called to bear witness to God's presence and to be the bearers of His love in the midst of our relationships and responsibilities. Synergy is the term often used by the Orthodox to express this active cooperation between God and human persons. St. Paul uses a form of this word in his first letter to the Corinthians when he says: "For we are co-workers (*synergoi*) with God, you are God's field, God's building" (1 Corinthians 3:9).

We are indeed called to be Gods "co-workers." Our relationship with God involves us in the process of divine reconciliation and healing. Again, St. Paul boldly expresses this profound conviction when he says: "God was in Christ reconciling Himself to the world and has given us the ministry of reconciliation" (2 Cor. 5:18). This bold affirmation is a very important conviction. It expresses the fact that we are not only valuable to God, but the Triune God also calls us to join with Him in the process of salvation. Synergy begins with our personal cooperation with God for the sake of our own relationship with Him. But, we know that our growth in holiness is not a private process. We are not saved in isolation. We grow in our relationship with God in the company of others and within the world. So, we are ultimately involved with God for the salvation of others and the whole world.

This perspective in no way seeks to diminish God as our Savior and as the giver of salvation. We believe that God is all-powerful and self-sufficient. These are among the most basic characteristics of God. Yet, the story of Mary as well as other stories from the New Testament and the stories of the saints throughout the ages remind us that God calls us to join with Him, not only for our own salvation, but also as His partners in the work of salvation of the world. We affirm that God calls us to share in the process of salvation as His friends and collaborators. With the Virgin Mary and all the saints as our guides, every faithful follower of Christ can share in the divine plan of salvation for all.[22]

Persons who have grown to a mature degree of authenticity, knowingly or not, become vehicles of healing and peace. In a growing relationship with the Author of Life, they naturally help others relate more genuinely to the love of God already present in their lives. St. Gregory calls these persons "peacemakers" (cf. Mt. 5:9). These are the persons, he says,

> who imitate the love of God for humankind, who reveal in their own lives the characteristics of God's activity. The Lord and giver of good things completely annihilates anything that is without affinity and foreign to goodness. This work He also directs for you. Namely, to cast out hatred and abolish war, to exterminate envy and banish strife, to get rid of hypocrisy, and to extinguish from within resentment of injuries which linger in the heart.[23]

A Noble Vocation

I have come to believe that there are at least three qualities that are necessary for this dynamic of a loving relationship to be fully present among human persons, especially those who follow Christ. Firstly, unconditional honesty is necessary for a recognition or appreciation of the other's unique mystery. Secondly, profound courage is required for loving surrender to the other. And thirdly, there must be a trusting willingness to receive the other. These three qualities: recognition, surrender, and reception are essential for authentic relationships.

When we reflect on the mystery of the Trinity, we see that the Father, for example, recognizes the otherness of the Son and surrenders to Him in order to receive Him within the ineffable mystery of their infinite love. Outside of time and space, well beyond our capacity to fully understand, each person of the Trinity – Father, Son, and Holy Spirit – abides in the other without confusion in this manner.

Impossible as it may seem, God calls human persons to this same noble vocation, albeit in our human, limited, manner. We grow ever closer toward the mystery of who we are called to be the more we recognize, surrender to and receive the love of the living God. At the same time, we are called to recognize, surrender to and receive the mystery of other human persons, as well as the reality of ourselves and creation in the presence of God. This dynamic process offers us true life and ultimately leads to greater levels of authentic relationship with God, others, creation, and self.

Persons in Community

Human persons are meant to be in communion with other persons. Authentic human life requires relationships with others. A relationship with God cannot be separated from relationships with other persons. As human persons, we share a common origin in God's creative love and we share a common goal in God's transfiguring love. We are bound together in God and are by nature social persons. We are not meant to live our lives in isolation from others. Rather, we are meant to be in relationship with others. "For nothing is so characteristic of our nature," says St. Basil, "than to relate with one another, to need one another, and to love our fellow human persons."[24]

Let us remember that our faith has always affirmed an intimate bond between all persons rooted in the very act of God in creation. We all share the same human nature regardless of gender, race, nationality or economic status. God is the Creator and Father of all. Archbishop Anastasios of Albania says:

> This view is repeatedly emphasized in the New Testament (Mt. 6:9, 23:9 and Rom 1:7 are some examples) and is directly related to the conviction that all people, without exception, are God's children and are therefore brothers and sisters...All of humanity is thus one great, undivided and unified whole, the core of whose existence is the living Trinitarian God: 'One God and Father of us all, who is above all and through all and in all' (Eph. 4:6).[25]

This need for others is certainly not a result of personal weakness. Rather, it is inherent in our very being. While each of us is unique, each of us is created for relationship with others. Just as we did not create ourselves we also cannot live by ourselves. To be in relationship with others is an essential characteristic of our human nature. A loving orientation of person to person is natural. It is essential to our identity. As the Trinity is a communion of persons, the human person is created for life in communion with others.

Again, Christ bore witness to this truth throughout His ministry. The call of the Lord to the first disciples was an invitation to be in relationship with Him and with all those whom He called. The first followers of Christ were not called to a life of discipleship to live in isolation. They each were called to be a member of a community of believers centered upon Christ. From the very beginning, the disciples were part of a "new family," a community of faith.

This process has continued throughout the life of the Church from the time of the first disciples. Every believer who is called by Christ to be His follower is also called to be a member of His people which is the Church. The Sacrament of Baptism expresses the bond not only with Christ but also with all those who are united with Christ. Moreover, when we gather for the Eucharist and receive Holy Communion, we do as members of the Body of Christ. This is beautifully expressed in the fact that we all share from the same sanctified bread and wine from the same cup. The Church is a community of faith in which our relationship with the Triune God and with others is deepened.

With the above in mind, it is easy to appreciate how this "new family" in Christ transcends the bonds of race, of blood, of social position, of background, and gender. It is a family in which each person is accepted and in which each finds affirmation and healing from fellow believers. When we seek to live our lives "in Christ," we see one another as brother and sister, and strive to "bear each other's burdens" (Gal. 6:2). It is a family that is founded upon the saving acts of the Triune God, "who calls us out of darkness into His marvelous light (1 Pet 2:9)."

Authentic human relationships are those which nurture love, compassion and mercy, as these bear witness to the ineffable love of God. Authentic relationships are those that sensitize us to appreciate the needs of another. Like God's relationship with us, our relationships with others are meant to be expressions of love that heal, reconcile, and promote growth. It is through isolation from God and others that we stagnate as human persons. To be a person is to be in relationship with others. It is in communion with God and others that we grow in our human identity.

The relationship among persons is also expressed through the blessings that each of us receive. Essential to our distinctive personality is the fact that each of us is blessed with particular talents and abilities. These bear witness to our distinctive identity, and are to be received with thanksgiving and cultivated with humility as blessings from God. At the same time, the blessings that each of us receive are not for us alone! With God as the source of our blessings, we receive them in order to share them with others. It is through the sharing of our gifts with others that we grow in our imitation of Christ.

St. Basil reminds us of the importance of sharing our gifts when he says:

> No single person is capable of receiving all the spiritual gifts, but the Holy Spirit is given accord-

> ing to the faith that is in each one. And so, in the life together what is given secretly to one becomes the common gift of all the others. The one who receives each of the Spirit's gifts, whether it be knowledge, wisdom, faith or any other gift, receives it as much for the sake of the others as for his own sake.[26]

There is a profound connection between our relationship with God and our relationship with others. If they are authentic, the relationships are reflective of the same love. This is the reason why our Lord affirmed the connection between the love of God and the love of the neighbor. He says: "You shall love the Lord your God with your whole heart, with your whole soul and with all of your mind and you shall love your neighbor as yourself" (Mt. 22:37-39). Our loving relationship with God requires a healthy love for self and for others.

St. Dorotheus of Gaza provides us with an important paradigm for authentic relationships. He speaks powerfully about the interrelationship of our love of God and others when he says:

> Suppose the circle is the world, and that the center of the circle is God. Leading from the edge of the circle to its center are a number of lines, and these represent the paths or ways of life that people can follow. In their desire to draw near to God, the holy ones advance along these lines towards the middle of the circle, so that the further they go, the nearer they approach to one another as well as to God. The closer they come to God the closer they come to one another, and the closer they come to one another, the closer they come to God. Such is the nature of love.[27]

The relationships among followers of Christ are also meant to be a constant reminder of the importance of the deep relationship which each of us has with every member of the human family.

Regardless of circumstances or of belief, our faith reminds us that the same loving and merciful God created everyone. Each person, regardless of ethnic origin, sex, or economic background is part of the same human family that the Creator has fashioned. Moreover, each of us has been united with God in a very intimate way through the humanity that Christ has shared. Not all may recognize these fundamental truths. Yet, the follower of Christ seeks to affirm them and to live by them. We are called by Christ not simply to love those who are like us! Love implies respect for the dignity and value of the other. We are called to love one another as Christ loves us. Ultimately, these relationships of love contribute to the salvation of the whole world. The loving person is a healer and reconciler.

The Church, this new family in Christ, therefore, is related to all humanity. Yes, God calls all to His love and salvation. God wills that all experience His love. While each person is free to choose God and His love, no one is meant to be left behind. The Church bears witness to God's love for all persons. The Church bears witness to His intention to draw all persons to His communion. Moreover, the Church is always an icon of God's love for all and the sign of the inherent bond which exists among all people who share a common Father.

Speaking of the relationship between the Church and the entire world, Archbishop Anastasios says,

> Just as the life of Christ, the new Adam, has global consequences, so too, the life of His mystical body, the Church, has worldwide importance and impact. Everything the Church is and everything it does concerns all of humanity, throughout the entire world. As an indication and 'icon' of the kingdom, the Church is the axis of cohesion in the entire process of 'recapitulation' – the process by which all things become united in Christ. It is on behalf of all people that the Church acts, offers the Divine Eucharist, and praises God. It radiates the glory of the living Lord throughout the entire world.[28]

Relationships that Seek To Heal and To Restore

There are essentially two types of relationships. In very simple terms, one expression may be identified as our fundamental vocation to grow in "authentic" relationship. And, the other, we may identify as toxic "inauthentic" or "distorted" relationship. When our relationships are essentially authentic (or perhaps more correctly, are in the process of becoming ever more authentic), we find that we are moving more toward the mystery of the person we have been created to be while simultaneously growing in relationship with the living God of love. Over time, this is characterized by change and growth.

There are also observable consequences and fruits of this growth confirming its genuineness. As we become ever more the persons we are called to be, we become more spiritually whole and psychologically healthy. With ever deepening maturity, we more deeply abide in God. Through the love of God, we come to experience forgiveness and healing. Truly, God reveals Himself to us and through us.

The New Testament and the lives of the saints are filled with examples that illustrate this process and inspire us. This is not a new teaching. In fact, our Lord stated His primary mission quite clearly: "I have come to give life, life in abundance" (Jn. 10:10). This simple declaration has much to teach us about the Kingdom and the reign of God who loved us first.

These words should have profound ramifications in every aspect of our lives, every minute of the day. They inspire us to ongoing mindfulness and discipline while relying on the ever-present tender mercy of God. They can guide us in cultivating our life more genuinely with God, ourselves, others and creation. The Church was established by the Lord Jesus Christ through the Holy Spirit in order to cultivate and share this "abundant life" not simply with fellow believers but also with the whole world.

In contrast, when we engage in relationships from an essentially in-authentic foundation, we are in some manner remaining self-centered and pre-occupied. The "other," whether it be God or a human person, cannot be genuinely recognized and received due to this distraction and self-absorption. This promotes a toxic, ongoing distortion of relationships, as well as our own delusions of reality, thus making it ever more difficult for us to receive the love of the One who loved us first.

Surely, there are countless in-authentic choices we may make everyday in relationships. Too many of these indeed, feel pleasurable. Many of these pleasing choices even promote a kind of " sick life" of their own, but in the end, these are counterfeit. Moreover, it is very easy to live an entirely false life. A false life may sometimes be exciting, titillating and/or intoxicating. It can even be "shared" to some degree by others trapped in the same type of false reality. It is a dynamic that parades itself as life, but is not authentic as it does not lead us toward the Author of Life.

Sin cannot support authentic life. Sadly, on a daily basis, we sin whenever we avoid seeking to recognize others for whom they are in the presence of God. Whenever we may find ourselves treated in this manner, we may be easily provoked to protect ourselves from being falsely defined. In sometimes overt and at other times in very subtle ways, every incident of in-authentic relating is experienced as toxic and life-effacing to the profoundest depth of our sense of being. This life-effacing dynamic is painful and may in certain extreme situations be experienced as a kind of de-personalization[29] and hence, de-realization. Even more tragically, the effects of this toxic, in-authentic relating builds layer upon layer within our deepest assumptions of ourselves to the point where we may even fool ourselves into thinking these false definitions of ourselves are actually true.

With this in mind, we can see how easy it is for human persons to "miss the mark" in relationships. Our immediate protective reaction to even a singular perceived aggression of false relating all too often originates from the apparent source of the experienced injury. We somehow "forget" or "neglect" to respond authentically as a way to help correct or at least curtail the aggression. Instead of responding in a manner that bears witness to the truth of whom we are called to be in the presence of God, we may more easily seek "an eye for an eye."

Under these circumstances, it is far more difficult to seek responses that strive to heal and restore authentic relationship. Rather than the love-based dynamic of recognition, surrender and reception that serve as the foundation for healthy and genuine relationships, there are countless stridently self-centered ways we may respond with opposing reactions. These fear-based reactions include projection and defensiveness among others. All too easily, we add more "insult to injury" as we succumb to the temptation of over-compensating from a perceived threat to our identity. As a result, we can define and project ourselves in a manner that is not true to our genuine identity as sons and daughters of God. Our responses sorely "miss the mark."

At the same time, we also must recognize we can just as easily assert ourselves falsely even without being threatened personally. The story in the Book of Genesis describing the "Fall" of humankind illustrates this. As the story tells us, Adam and Eve fell due to their willful submission to the temptation of striving to become god without God. They wanted to be "autonomous" individuals living apart from their Father and Creator.

It is sometimes difficult to discern whether a particular relationship, and our conduct within it, is truly life-giving, or whether they are distracting, seductive, or counterfeit. Discernment may take time. In the process of discernment, we should remember that the common denominator of all in-authentic relationships is that they are toxic and life-effacing. They do not enhance life and they do not aid in holiness. They promote their own kind of poisonous intoxication, delusion or "spell." At the same time, they distance us from the "one thing necessary." Jesus warns, in very simple terms, of the danger of being distracted when He says: "where your treasure is, there will your heart be also" (Mt. 6:21).

The false treasures to which we become attached become our personal false gods. They become idols. Given enough time, our other relationships eventually will exist to serve this "false divinity." Whenever our priorities are skewed by an allegiance to a false god, we automatically relate in-authentically with our own selves, God, others and creation. The more in-authentic we are, the more we risk promoting a parallel toxic and life-effacing dynamic in all our relationships. In some manner or other, consciously or not, we would choose to abuse others, ourselves and/or creation rather than relinquish our attachment to our false god.

Relationships that are essentially distorted and in-authentic, are also toxic and life-effacing. They are also abusive in some way. Every expression of abuse – such as physical, sexual, financial, psychological intimidation – essentially targets the soul. One of the most destructive spiritual and psychological forces perpetrated against human persons is invisibility. Invisibility targets the soul and the exploitation of this false message is a common weapon wielded by persons who abuse others.

To the very heart of one's soul, the loveless lies of invisibility are proclaimed: "you do not count…" "you do not measure up…" "you have no value!" One of the fundamental, spiritual consequences of abuse, including "non-physical" abuse committed through intimidation, neglect and abandonment, is the undermining of one's true sense of person and reality. This undermines our ability to relate authentically as it also severely weakens free will.

The Orthodox spiritual tradition affirms that human free will can never be completely eradicated. Healing begins whenever persons "re-member" who they are in the presence of God. This "re-membering" integrates us more fully in our true identity as unique sons and daughters of the loving God.

When lived in the presence of the love of the living God, our authentic relationships nurture us in "the life in abundance." This is often not an easy journey. This journey is not infrequently very dangerous. Nevertheless, the more we endeavor to relate authentically with ourselves, others and creation in the presence of God, the more possibility we have for being a vehicle for the presence and love of God.

This, of course, affects all aspects of our lives. As we strive to live within authentic relationships and to deepen our roots in Reality, we also enjoy an unexpected by-product. The more truthfully we recognize, surrender to and receive the love of the living God, the more God's mercy, forgiveness, healing, power and authority is personally made present to us, as well. The ancient Greek term for "authenticity" which is *authentia,* which also indicates authority, now takes on its distinctly personal, rich and life-giving Christian perspective. This term now bears witness to the new reality expressed through the Gospel of our Lord and Savior Jesus Christ.

Failures of Human Community

Sadly, it is very easy to discount the significance of our relational character. We are members of a society where the tendency towards isolation and de-personalization is very powerful. Work, school, errands, meetings, chores and the very hectic, distracting "business" of everyday contemporary life take their toll in diminishing relationships, and in keeping family and friends apart. If we do not live in a conscious and faithful manner, human "doing" and external appearance can undermine human "being" and authentic relationships with God and others. There are countless examples we can identify that points to this pattern.

For instance, many of us live in neighborhoods where we do not know our neighbor. Some of us live in apartment complexes where we have little contact with the other inhabitants. We often work in situations where isolation and competition at the expense of others ultimately undermines human relationships in the name of productivity and efficiency. We may shop at larger superstores or over the internet, and not at the local market where we may know the clerk. We can receive phone calls from telemarketers thousands of miles away and treat the caller like a non-person because she or he has interrupted our dinner. We can do our banking at a machine or even from home without a teller. And, sometimes, it is necessary that we conduct business with large educational institutions, government agencies or medical establishments where we are not known by our names. We are identified by our number! In many aspects of our lives, authentic engagement with other persons is sorely lacking.

These tendencies in our society contribute to our becoming ever-more de-sensitized to the plight of others around us. We can become increasingly self-absorbed in a manner that isolates us from the love of God. The more we pursue objectives that distract us from the "one thing necessary" (Lk. 10:42), the more our personal senses and sensibilities become increasingly deadened to perceiving the needs of our neighbor. We may see our neighbor with our eyes, but actually we are blind to appreciating the person for who he or she may be in the presence of God (1 Jn 4:20). The other person becomes a "thing." Therefore, we respond with a pitiful lack of love and sincere concern often rendering them invisible. What we do not realize is that usually a corresponding part of our own soul "dies" or becomes "hardened" or "frozen" as well. In that instant, we fail to grow in the mystery of the unique persons whom God intended us to become.

Our Lord has directed us, His followers, to not only love God but also to love our neighbor as we love ourselves. He reminds us that there is an indivisibility to authentic love. We cannot claim to love God unless we also love our neighbor and have a healthy love for self.

The word for neighbor in the Greek New Testament is *pleiseion*. This word conveys the idea of "the person who happens to be standing next to me." The neighbor may be a member of our own family, neighborhood, local community or larger society. He or she may share the same life with us. Or, the neighbor may be someone completely foreign to us. It may be a person who does not share our views, or our religious convictions. It may be a person who is not of the same race or nationality.

The spiritual flaw we hold in common is that in some manner we do not recognize the immediacy of the Lord's commandment that "we love our neighbor as we love ourselves" (cf. Mt. 22:39). Growing in authentic relationship with others in the presence of God pushes us beyond dead-ended and human-based definitions of status and superficial relationship. When we fail to recognize our neighbor, not only do we increasingly become less than our "true self" but also we fail to follow the command of our Lord. In an insidious manner, we drift further and further away from and become ever more cold to the presence of the Kingdom. The Lord says to us: "You are the salt of the earth. But, if salt loses its taste, with what can it be seasoned? It is no longer good for anything but to be thrown out and trampled underfoot" (Mt. 5:13). These words are a powerful affirmation of our responsibility. They are also a warning!

Truly, Christian communities are not immune from a distortion of relationship with others. We may speak of the importance of truly Christian communities where believers have a sense of a larger "family in Christ." Yet, we know that many of our parishes have the reputation for not being welcoming communities. There are parishes today, for example, where the lines are clearly drawn between old-timers and the new-comer. There are parishes which appear self-contained and unconcerned about witness and mission in their neighborhood and society. How do these Christians understand the "neighbor"? What is the characteristic of the "salt" of these Christians and their parishes?

Perhaps we all know of similar situations of human division that reflect these failings. The hallmarks of contemporary society's spiritual pathology as it vies for our unconditional allegiance include a number of unfortunate characteristics. These may include the unbridled drive for success and power; materialism and consumerism; mobility and technology in the service of greed, power, and entertainment. So many of these can easily undermine the fostering of genuine relationships. When these tendencies predominate, human persons are somehow pre-defined and objectified as not valuable. Whenever human persons engage each other with these characteristics, relationships are less than authentic and life-giving. Rather, they become life-effacing.

It is possible to enjoy many of the advances of this technological age and still be authentic. However, in our society we must strive to become far more discerning with regard to the potential dangers of the life-effacing degradation of genuine relationships. Perhaps we need to affirm more intentionally the inherent value of human relationships in our society. Perhaps we need to become all the more committed to contributing to those activities that foster and strengthen human relationships in our homes, parishes, schools and businesses. Truly, as followers of the Lord who are members of this society, we need to affirm constantly the inherent value of personhood and our obligation to treat others as Christ would.

Our relationship with God is meant to be nurtured, guided and supported through the relationships that we have with one another. We are conciliar persons. St Basil reminds us that we are created for relationships with others when he says,

> Surely everyone knows that human persons are social creatures and for that reason are not made for a solitary and uncivilized life. Nothing is better suited to our nature then to have continual relationships, to seek out each other, and to love one's own kind. The Lord asks no more than the fruit of the seed He has implanted in us, when He says: 'A new commandment I give to you, that you love one another' (John 13:34).[30]

By virtue of the fact that every one of us is created by the same Triune God, there is a foundational relationship between us that is established in the very structure of creation. Whether we recognize it or not, the Triune God has "knit us together" in His love (Eph. 4:16). Each of us shares the same Heavenly Father. And, this Father offers His love to each of us. He shares the rest of creation with us. As persons dependent upon the Father, we share the same earth, the same air, the same water. Truly, "the heavens declare the greatness of the Lord and the works of His hands, the firmament proclaims" (Ps. 19:1). Every aspect of this creation is a blessing meant to inspire our love for God. The creation is also a means of communion between ourselves and God, and an essential means of communion among ourselves in the presence of God.

A number of contemporary theologians have made an important distinction which can help us to understand the significance of the person in community. In our common language, many of us use these terms interchangeably. Yet, these theologians have pointed to a deeper meaning for both. This is the distinction between "person" and "individual." Theologians such as Archbishop Anastasios

Yannoulatos, Metropolitan John Zizioulas, Metropolitan Maximos Aghiorgoussis, Bishop Kallistos Ware, Fr. Dumitru Staniloe, Oliver Clement and Christos Yannaras have all addressed this distinction in one way or anther in their writings.

These theologians frequently speak of the "individual" as one who is isolated, self-contained, self–absorbed or "cut off" from others. The individual is somehow alienated from conscious communion with God and others. The "individual" lives as if he or she is not intimately bound to and influenced by God and others. This individualistic life is ultimately something less than fully human.

On the other hand, a "person" is a unique human being who is engaged in conscious, active, growing and healthy relationships with God and others in the midst of creation. The Greek word for person is *prosopon*. It means "facing forward." Likewise, the Latin word for person is *persona*, which means "sounding through." Both terms, while not interchangeable, imply a living relationship with another reality. Mindful of the Trinitarian relationships of the three divine Persons, we could say that the human being is truly a person when he or she is open to another in love. Such a person is truly living in a healthy relationship.

Certainly, we live in a time and place where there are many forces which push us towards an individualistic understanding of the human person. The many pressures of life often move us toward an isolationism which diminishes the significance and importance of the relationships with God and others, relationships which are essential to the meaning of personhood. The frenzied demands of life today, as well as the characteristics of large institutions and religious extremism, manifest a relationship that often depersonalize us and distort our true identity.

In the face of these tendencies towards human isolationism and depersonalization, we need all the more to deepen our understanding of the human person as one who is called to be a person in a loving relationship with God and with others and with the creation.

This dynamic calling consists of two dimensions which, at first, might appear to be contradictory. The first is that we are called to grow in the mystery of becoming unique human persons. Secondly, we are called to communion with God. Both of these vocations may appear to be contradictory. In reality, they are mutually inter-dependent.

Every human person is unique and, therefore, unrepeatable. While each of us share in the common humanity, each of us is a distinctive person with our own characteristics. The recent advances in biology bear witness to the distinctiveness of each of us. In a very real sense, each of us is constantly deepening our understanding of our "mysterious" self. We will always be exploring the depths of who we are! We are constantly in the process of becoming ourselves in relationship to God and others! Along with the Psalmist, we thank God and proclaim: "I will praise you, for I am fearfully and wonderfully made (Ps. 139:14)."

This means that our true growth as a person requires that we rid ourselves of every characteristic which diminishes or distorts our true identity. This includes features of our life that lack love. It includes everything which is false and hypocritical.

Our ultimate identity originates in God. And so, in order to further discern who we are, we continuously courageously surrender ourselves to relationship with the loving God. Growing in our relationship with God, we also become more ourselves. Furthermore, as we mature, through the grace of the Holy Spirit, we become more god-like. At the same time, we surrender our preconceived notions of ourselves. This process is echoed in the words of St. Paul: "When I was a child, I spoke as a child, I thought as a child; but when I became a man, I put away childish things" (I Cor. 13:11). We do so as we pray: "Your will not my will be done."

At the same time, the growth in authentic relationship requires that human persons progress not only toward intimacy with God, but also with others. As we receive the other, we also surrender our preconceived notions about the other person we are receiving and ourselves, as well. Growing in authentic relationship, even with our own selves, challenges us to trust and surrender ourselves to God, to another.

These perspectives have a particular importance for Christians.

Each of us is called to follow Our Lord in a manner that is deeply personal. As His disciples, each of us maintains his or her unique personal identity. Each human person is an unrepeatable mystery. We each have our own experiences, our own gifts and our own responsibilities. We each have our own unique spiritual journey. Through our response to Christ, we manifest the fundamental relationship to God which is rooted in our human identity.

Yet, at the same time, we are always disciples in relationship with others. At our Baptism, we are united to Christ. Simultaneously, we are united to all those who are also related to Christ through baptism. We become part of the Church which is the Body of Christ. We become part of a community of believers. Our discipleship is one in which we are not simply guided to the Father through Christ in the Spirit. Our discipleship is such that each of us is knit together with everyone who is in Christ. We are part of a human community that manifests itself in the community of faithful people.

There is an ancient axiom that says, "a solitary Christian is no Christian." This means that the very definition of Christian implies not only a relationship with Christ but also a relationship with others who are also faithful followers of Christ. Salvation is a process that takes place in relationship with God and with others. St. Paul reminds us, we are "one body in Christ" (1 Cor.12:13-17). We are "members of one another" (Rom. 12:5). We are also called to "bear each others burdens" so to "fulfill the law of Christ" (Gal. 6:2).

We must bear in mind that, as vital as the content of the faith (*pistis*) is, the Greek word for faith is not simply a noun. "Faith" in Greek is also a verb. When used as a verb, *pistis* often can be better translated as "trust." Trust by definition causes us to move out of ourselves, and beyond ourselves, in order to more truly become ourselves. Jesus calls us His followers and to place our trust in God who calls us to be truly His daughters and sons.

St Gregory of Sinai says to us:

> Become what you already are,

> Find Him who is already yours,
> Listen to Him who never ceases speaking to you,
> Possess Him who already possesses you!³¹

Persons in Creation

Our relationship with the Triune God and with one another always takes place within the context of the created world. Each of us shares in the created reality. We are not simply spiritual beings. Rather, we are spiritual-material persons. While we affirm a distinctive quality and dignity of the human person, we are never detached from the rest of the created reality. This means that the process of salvation in Christ has a cosmic dimension. Human persons share in the reality of the entire creation

The creation is the gift of the good and loving God. God's gift is fundamentally good. Although this creation is prone to distortion, both because of its createdness and because of human sin, it remains fundamentally valuable and "very good" (Gen 1:31) because it has its origin in God. The creation bears witness to His providence and love.

Moreover, the importance of the creation is also rooted in the reality of Christ's coming. By uniting himself with our humanity, the Word of God established a profound relationship not only with our human nature but also with the entire created order. The fact is that God entered into the material world in a profound manner in the person of Jesus Christ. In assuming our humanity, God in Christ took upon Himself our full humanity which meant our physical dimension. He truly shared in our flesh and blood, and all it means to be fully human!

In addition to this, Jesus frequently referred to aspects of creation in His teachings (e.g. Mt 7:6f). He used elements of creation to reveal His divine power (e.g. Jn 2:1-11). The one who created and fashioned the world truly entered into it for our salvation and for the salvation of the entire creation. The ultimate transfiguration of the entire cosmos is already prefigured not only in the lives of the faithful but also in the material of the Eucharist, the icons, and the relics of the saints.

St John Chrysostom speaks about the gift of creation when he says:

> The creation is beautiful and harmonious, and God has made it all just for your sake. He has made it beautiful, grand and rich, He has made it capable of satisfying all your needs, to nourish your body and also to develop the life of your soul by leading it towards the knowledge of himself, all this for your sake... For your sake, He has made the sky beautiful with stars. He has embellished it with sun and moon for your sake, so that you can take pleasure in it and be enriched by it.[32]

St. John reminds us of the relationship between the human person and the rest of the material creation. With this observation in mind, four affirmations are especially important.

First of all, the creation is a gift of God to be honored and treasured. Every aspect of creation is a blessing meant to inspire our love for the Creator and to draw us more closely to him, and to one another. If the human person is truly the crown of creation, then all the physical world is provided by God for our goodness and to assist us in our salvation. This creation is offered to us as a gift. It is meant to remind us of the goodness and power of God, our Creator. Fr. Dumitru Staniloae says: "We shall only understand the character of the world when we think of it as a gift or present. The whole world ought to be regarded as the visible part of a universal and continuing sacrament, and all man's activity as sacramental, divine communion."[33]

Patriarch Bartholomew stresses,

> the belief that every creature of God created for communion with human beings is good when it is received with thanksgiving (I Tim. 4:3-4) leads to respect for creation out of respect for its Creator. However, it does not fashion an idol out of creation itself. A person who loves the Creator of

a given work will neither be disrespectful toward it nor maliciously harm it. Yet, at the same time, that person will surely not worship it and disregard the Creator (Rom. 1:21). Rather, by honoring it, one honors its Creator.[34]

Second, the Orthodox Church makes constant use of the elements of the physical world in worship. Bread and wine, water and oil, fruits and flowers, are but a few of the many elements of creation which are taken up by the Church in its worship. Indeed, the icons of the Lord, Mary and the saints are composed of elements of creation. In blessing and offering the matter of creation, the Church affirms that the things of the earth have their origin with God. The physical world possesses intrinsic value. It can truly be a vehicle of His presence and a sign of His goodness.

Third, the physical creation establishes a special bond between human persons. We all share in this common inheritance from God's generosity. We all have inherited in the physical world a common blessing from the ultimate Source of all things. When viewed as a precious gift, the Creation is not something that we can truly possess in a selfish and self-centered manner. In receiving the Creation as a gift, each of us has the obligation to be true stewards of God's creation and to share this creation with others. For those with eyes to see, the physical world provides us with a profound means of communion with the Creator and with one another. Patriarch Bartholomew while promoting this teaching also offers a sober warning:

> *The world is not meant to be used by humans for their own purpose, but it is the means whereby humans come into relationship with God. If humans change this use into egocentric, greedy exploitation, into oppression and destruction of nature, then humanity's own vital relationship with God is denied and refuted, a relationship predestined to continue into eternity.*[35]

Our growth in holiness takes place within the context of the created world. Salvation also has its cosmic dimension. Human persons are not saved from the world but in and through the created world. The soul is not saved separately from the body, but rather together with the body. The whole person, body and soul, is meant to share in the process of deification beginning with the relationships and responsibilities of this life. Growth in holiness does not draw us away from the creation. The physical world is not by nature an obstacle to our growth in holiness. Far from rejecting the body and the rest of the material creation, we look upon the physical world as the work of God and the medium through which the divine is manifest.

Speaking especially of the dignity of the human body, St. Cyril of Jerusalem says:

> Look within yourself. From your own nature you can learn something of your Maker. There is nothing to be ashamed of in your body. If you are in control of your members, they are not in the slightest evil.... Our limbs do not cause us to sin, but the wrong use of them does...
>
> Look at your Maker. Admire your wise Creator. The greatest and beauty of His creatures will help you to contemplate Him....Those who despise the body should keep quiet: they despise Christ Himself who made it![36]

Most of the icons of the saints depict them in an historical setting. This is an important observation. Yes, it is true that the saint is pictured in a manner that appears to express his or her transfiguration. Likewise, there is sometimes a symbolic expression of the saint's particular ministry or task in life. The broader context of the saint usually depicts him or her within a specific historical time and place. Sometimes the saint is depicted in the company of others. In fact, some saints are depicted with their pets or other animals. Quite clearly, the saints who dwell with the Lord in glory are related in a positive way to their historical context through the icon. The icon is a clear reminder that the saint grew in holiness within the context of the responsibilities and obligations of daily life. The icon is also a reminder that life is meant to be lived in harmony with God's creation.

Finally, each believer is meant to be a priest of creation (1 Pet 2:5). In every aspect of our life, we have the opportunity to remember the acts of God and to offer back to the Father the creation as an act of praise and thanksgiving. We receive graciously what has been freely given to us. And, we offer back in thanksgiving the fruit of our human labor. The entire creation, good from the beginning, is related to the reality of the Incarnation. The ultimate transfiguration of the entire cosmos has already begun in the lives of the faithful, in the Eucharist, in the icons, and in the relics of the saints. Archbishop Anastasios says,

> Human beings have a vital need to be in a koinonia of love, not only with the rest of humanity but also with the world of nature and the entire universe. If we continue to abuse nature rather than to 'use' nature, there is a danger that the development of our technology will lead us to terrifying feats of self-destruction… It is time we understood that nature is something sacred. It does not lie outside the sphere of the Holy Spirit's activity.[37]

When we correctly see the creation as God's blessing, we must be especially troubled by the abuse of the environment. In many places, the rivers, lakes and seas are polluted by the irresponsible disposal of poisonous waste. And, this pollution has contributed to the destruction of fish and animal life. This pollution has contaminated drinking water. This pollution has contributed to climate change that profoundly affects the entire environment. In other places, natural resources have been abused, needlessly destroyed, or horded. In too many situations, the good earth, the gift of God, has been turned into an unhealthy and inhospitable home for the human family and for other living creatures. Greed and selfishness are often at the root of this tragic transformation. This tragic transformation is a threat to the quality of life itself. Patriarch Bartholomew powerfully reminds us that

> the final purpose of creation is not its use or abuse for humankind's individual pleasure, but something far more sublime and sacred. It is from these points, then, that the pastoral reasons for the Church's concern for the natural environment emanate. For us Orthodox, every destruction of the natural environment caused by humanity constitutes an offense against the Creator Himself and arouses a sense of sorrow. In relation to the degree to which people are responsible for their actions, *metanoia* – a radical change of course – is demanded for us all. For this reason, each human act that contributes to the destruction of the natural environment must be regarded as a very serious sin. We are talking here about a renewed ethos that must be taught to our faithful. Our faithful must become sensitized to the gravity of this sin and to the need to espouse a corresponding ethos. People must cease regarding themselves as *proprietors of nature* and understand their mission as *priests of creation* who have as their duty the *anaphora* or offering up of the material world to the Creator. In this new ethos, the liturgical and the ascetic tradition of the Church can be of assistance to its faithful.[38]

There is another abuse that we cannot overlook. This is the abuse of the human body which has become so prevalent in our society. The misuse of drugs, alcohol, food, sexuality, and various compulsive behaviors tends to lead to an insidious and progressive devaluation of the human body. Eventually, the body is treated, either consciously or unconsciously, with a subtle contempt and disregard. All of this can reflect in many persons a loss of values and meaning in life.

Followers of Christ have an obligation to speak with integrity and with humility about the value of the creation as a gift of the good and loving God. We cannot profess faith in the Triune God who is *philanthropos* without at the same time affirming that the world, the physical creation, is a gift and blessing given to us from Him. It is a sacred bond which unites human persons and relates them to all of life. At a time when the value of the human body is diminished, we must affirm that God creates it and that it too, is called to share in the process of salvation. We must remind all believers that we are called to be faithful stewards of the physical as well as the spiritual blessings of God.

We have the profound obligation to treasure the human body and the entire creation. We treasure the human body through the respect we show for it both in life and in death. We treasure the creation through the proper use of our limited natural resources. We treasure the creation through the thoughtful construction of church buildings, monasteries, places of business, schools and homes. Each time we bless our bodies and all the elements of creation, we give thanks to God and we affirm the value of the material world. As we bless and treasure the creation, we express God's healing and reconciliation for the entire world.

Conclusion: Some Practical Observations on Authentic Relationships

Jesus instructs His friends to "Seek first His Kingdom and His righteousness" (Mt. 6:33). With this directive, the Lord reminds us that every one of us is called to be the God-centered person that we are. The more Christians faithfully strive to live in accordance with the gospel of Christ, the more aware we become of every aspect of life being rooted in the presence of the One God who abides eternally in community of three Persons. As we more intentionally participate in this ineffable mystery, we are enabled by the loving God to become increasingly aware of the divinely established pattern of relationship mysteriously and lovingly embedded in creation in infinite ways.

Knowingly or not, the more faithfully we strive through our relationships to bear witness to the will and love of God, the more these serve life. The more we grow in our vocation as unique sons and daughters of the most high God by relating as truthfully as we are able with everyone and everything in our lives through God's mercy, the more holy we also become. Indeed, our relationships mysteriously even turn out to be vehicles for the Author of Life to make Himself known. Hence, our relationships become ever more life-giving, as we grow closer to God. Jesus declares His fundamental mission to the world: "I have come to give life, life in abundance" (Jn. 10:10) Receiving and growing in His abundant life is not easy for most of us, nevertheless, it is still our call to "follow Him."

When our relationships are "inauthentic," in other words, when we engage in relationships in ways that essentially serve lesser priorities and agenda, then our side of the relationship, inevitably, through time will become life-effacing. Eventually, knowingly or not, through our in-authentic relationships, we will be distracting others as well as cutting ourselves off from relating with the Author of Life. This occurs, primarily, because our lesser priorities are serving us as false gods, as idols. Given that idols are not the personal, real God, it is impossible for them to bestow true Life. Actively pursuing these false gods sets up, in time, a toxic dynamic that insidiously seeks to poison true life within a person and his or her relationships.

This makes it all the more important to ask ourselves frequently: "how do we understand and take part in our relationships; are they authentic?" We must, first of all, strive to avoid a serious misunderstanding and misapplication of the term "authentic." Striving to be "authentic" does not give a person license to engage in self-centered indulgence at the expense of others. For some people, self-absorption and self-indulgence may be the real underlying motivation for "being true to oneself." These manifestations of a pseudo-honesty more accurately reflect the sin of pride. According to the spiritual tradition of the Church, pride can be described as the want to become God without God. We are not accountable to "reality" which is our faithful abiding in the saving presence of the love of the living God as well as all of His creation. Instead, we live in the delusion that "it is all about us."

Fr. Dumitru Staniloae describes the danger of us succumbing to this fatally erroneous belief when he says that "we can be tempted to accentuate a certain tendency we have to affirm ourselves beyond our own proper limits and, thus, to leave out of account both other human beings and God, from whom we have both our existence and the possibility of enriching our experience. Were we to succumb to this temptation, we would tear to pieces our common human nature."[39]

The sin of pride is inauthentic. It distracts us from our true vocation which is to become the sons and daughters of the living God. Pride promotes our delusion that we are the center of the universe. If we are at the center of the universe, then there is no chance for a genuine relationship with God, other human persons, creation, even our own selves because we cannot know ourselves outside these relationships. When we are the center of our own universe, all other persons, both divine and human, essentially become mere objects to be manipulated in accordance with our own whims and selfish purposes. Pride, therefore, in the context of human relationship is in-authentic as it is profoundly toxic and life-effacing.

Authenticity may be understood as a dynamic quality of our life that witnesses to unconditional honesty with oneself in the presence of God. It reflects a kind of radical integrity. This dynamic is "radical" in the sense that its focus applies to the very root of our being. This process is also "radical" because it cannot be defined by fallen human convention. When we are engaged in authentic relationships, there is a coherence of personal being and action. While maintaining a healthy respect for personal privacy and confidentiality, there are, nevertheless, absolutely no secrets in the lives of those persons who relate authentically and live a life expressing radical integrity. There is no distinction between what we say and what we do; between who we are and how we live. Our "yes" truly means "yes"; our "no" truly means "no" (Mt. 5:37). Again, let me stress here, there are absolutely no secrets!

Persons whose lives consistently demonstrate this kind of radical honesty or integrity in its fullness may have been granted the gift of "purity of heart." The Lord teaches in the Beatitudes:

"blessed are the pure in heart, for they shall see God" (Mt. 5:8). Purity of Heart is a prerequisite for being in complete relationship with God. Jesus urges His followers to earnestly seek after this.

Fr. Laurence, Founder of the Monastery of New Skete says:

> All of [this] leads us to the question of how to purify our hearts. The fathers directed their followers to live 'Christianly,' i.e., to live virtuously, to live a good life … We try to live in a way that puts our Christianity into practice, in a way that makes it real, and not just some form of hypocrisy!!! All of our attempts to live a good life, to cleanse ourselves of our bad habits and sinful aspects, is called in Greek, *praxis*, which means 'practice.' *Praxis* is to notice how we live, what we are like, and to take the steps necessary to correct our life, to make our life more and more as it should be. This *praxis* then leads to *theoria* sooner or later, depending on our progress in this self-purification process. The Christian life, lived correctly, authentically, leads to a knowledge of God, to contemplation on a mystical level.[40]

The more authentic our relationships become, the more they increasingly become vehicles that facilitate healing and/or greater levels of wholeness. In ways that we are not usually aware, our relating genuinely bears witness to the saving love of God in the specific situation. This presents an invitation and opportunity for those engaged to respond likewise.

Conversely, people are injured spiritually and psychologically primarily through in-authentic relationships. In countless ways, we inflict injury upon ourselves, one another and creation through sins such as: malice, pride, lust for power, greed, well-guarded ignorance and studied naiveté, resentment and gross indifference to the plight of others. While admittedly these and other sins are exciting and titillating, they also promote a toxic, life-effacing dynamic. To be sure, various expressions of this life-effacing dynamic can be found in our homes, the workplace, our parishes, through the culture and in our society.

Unfortunately, all too often a toxic, life-effacing dynamic occurs which promotes one non-truth after another until a whole miniature universe is created in which persons find themselves trapped. Other times, the "trap" is far more subtle as when a self-serving, shaming non-truth may be combined in some manner with certain aspects of truth. This may be promoted quite cleverly. These situations usually present themselves to be "necessary," "for the greater good" and "for the sake of unity." This type of exploitation occurs among individual persons, groups of persons and by powerful persons in the name of institutions subjecting others. This last phenomenon especially and profoundly identifies the hypocrisy of our times.

Ignoring these sins will not make them go away. All too often, denial of such maladies actually feeds their malignant growth! These sins must be identified in order to unmask them. The "idolatry" must be named for what it is. Unmasking them, reveals them to the light, thus undermining their power. However, not unlike a deer vulnerable to being caught in the bright headlights of oncoming traffic, we, too, must not stare for too long or too closely into their depths once fully identified. Otherwise, we, too, risk being caught in an even stronger death hold.

Staring too long into the abyss of sin distracts us from our relationship with the loving God. Staring too long initiates another arguably more powerful and poisonous dynamic that leads us further away from authentic life and relationships. The spiritual wisdom of the Church instructs us to turn away from false gods and, instead, focus our gaze toward God for His help. Saint John of Kronstadt, who died in the early part of the twentieth century, speaks to the importance of seeking God in the face of sin. He says: "The challenge of our life is to be united with God, and sin completely prevents this. Therefore, flee from sin as from the destroyer of the soul. Because to be without God is death and not life. Let us always remember that our common Master calls us to union with Himself."[41]

St. Gregory of Nyssa offers us similar lifesaving advice. He tells us that the best way to protect the precious gift of our relationship with God is to faithfully "look to Him." It is a directive that is at least as important for us today as it was for his flock during the fourth century. He concludes this presentation with the following life-giving instruction:

> For this is the safest way to protect the good things you enjoy: Realize how much your Creator has honored you above all other creatures. He did not make the heavens in His image, nor the moon, the sun, the beauty of the stars or anything else which surpasses understanding. You alone are a reflection of eternal beauty, a receptacle of happiness, an image of the true light. And, if you look to Him, you will become what He is, imitating Him who shines within you, whose glory is reflected in your purity. Nothing in the entire creation can equal your grandeur. All the heavens can fit into the palm of the hand of God . . . Although He is so great that He can hold all creation in His palm, you can wholly embrace Him. He dwells in you.[42]

Notes

[1] St. Basil, *The Longer Rules*, 2.

[2] Cf. Kyriaki FitzGerald and Thomas FitzGerald, *Happy in the Lord: The Beatitudes for Everyday,* (Brookline, MA: Holy Cross Orthodox Press, 2000). 36; Dumitru Staniloe, *The Experience of God: Orthodox Dogmatic Theology, Volume 2. The World: Creation and Deification*, Ioan Ionita and Robert Barringer, trans., (Brookline: Holy Cross Orthodox Press, 2000), 74-80.

[3] St. Gregory of Nyssa, *On the Beatitudes*, Sermon 6.

[4] See Archbishop Demetrios Trakatellis, "Man Fallen and Restored in the Teachings of St. John Chrysostom," *Sobornost*, 4:10 (1964), 569-584.

[5] St. Macarius of Egypt, *Fifty Spiritual Homilies*.

The Human Person in Relationship 73

[6] Origen, *Principles*, 3,6.

[7] Archbishop Anastasios Yannoulatos, *Facing the World: Orthodox Christian Essays on Global Concerns*, (Crestwood, NY: St. Vladimir's Seminary Press, 2003), 58.

[8] Gregory the Theologian, *On Care for the Poor*, Oration 14:25.

[9] St. John Chrysostom, *On the Gospel of John*, Sermon 10.

[10] Patriarch Bartholomew I, "Beyond Arid Intellectualism," in *Cosmic Grace and Humble Prayer: The Ecological Vision of the Green Patriarch Bartholomew I*, John Chryssavgis, ed., (Grand Rapids, MI/Cambridge, U.K.: William B. Eerdmans Publishing Company, 2003), 206.

[11] St. Irenaeus, *Against Heresies*, 3:22:1; see also: St. Justin the Martyr, *Dialogue with Trypho*, 100.

[12] St. Gregory of Nyssa, *The Making of Man*, 18.

[13] Archbishop Anastasios, p. 163.

[14] Archbishop Anastasios, p. 60.

[15] St. Nicholas Cabasilas, *The Life in Christ*, 4.

[16] Patriarch Bartholomew I, "Encyclical Letter, September 1, 1994," in *Cosmic Grace and Humble Prayer*, p. 45.

[17] Kallistos Ware, "The Mystery of the Human Person," in *Sobornost* 3:1, 63.

[18] St. Irenaeus, *Against Heresies*, 4,20,7.

[19] St. Gregory of Nyssa, *On the Song of Songs*, Homily 2.

[20] Kallistos Ware, "Foreword" in Philip Sherrard, *Christianity: Lineaments of a Sacred Tradition*, (Brookline, MA: Holy Cross Orthodox Press, 1998), xxxi.

[21] St. Athanasius the Great, *On the Incarnation*, 54.

[22] St. Irenaeus, *Against Heresies*, 3:21:7.

[23] St. Gregory of Nyssa, *On the Beatitudes*, Homily 7

[24] St. Basil the Great, *The Long Rules*, Question III.

[25] Archbishop Anastasios, p. 59.

[26] St. Basil the Great, *Longer Rules*, 6

[27] St. Dorotheus of Gaza, *Instructions*, 6

[28] Archbishop Anastasios, p. 148.

[29] I am well aware that "de-personalization" is a clinical term used to identify a specific psychological phenomenon. My usage of this term does not exclude necessarily this understanding, yet it is used in a more general manner. This is because "de-personalization" from an Orthodox perspective also has profound spiritual implications as well.

[30] St. Basil the Great, *The Long Rule*, 3.

[31] St. Gregory of Sinai cited in Archbishop Paul of Finland, *The Faith We Hold* (Crestwood, NY: St. Vladimir's Seminary Press, 1980), 96.

[32] St. John Chrysostom, *Homily on Providence*, 7:2.

[33] Fr. Dumitru Staniloae, "The World as Gift and Sacrament of God's Love," *Sobornost* 5:9 (1969), 665.

[34] Patriarch Bartholomew, "Encyclical Letter, September 1, 1999," in *Cosmic Grace and Humble Prayer*, 57.

[35] Patriarch Bartholomew I, "Religion and Conservation," in *Cosmic Grace and Humble Prayer*, 148.

[36] St. Cyril of Jerusalem, *Catecheses*, 9,15; 12,26.

[37] Archbishop Anastasios, p. 37.

[38] Patriarch Bartholomew, "The Power of Joint Prayer and Action" in *Cosmic Grace and Humble Prayer,* 81.

[39] Staniloe, 69.

[40] Fr. Laurence, unpublished reflections on prayer.

[41] St. John of Kronstadt, *My Life in Christ*, 12

[42] St. Gregory of Nyssa, *On the Song of Songs*, 2

Appendix

Observations on Authentic Relationships: A Therapist's Revelation

This is a response to the question: "What is it that you do as an Orthodox Christian therapist?" This is offered with profound, loving gratitude to my friends and colleagues Patricia Finnegan, LICSW and Maxine Salvatore, Ph.D., who loved me so much, as to ask this question … and who tenderly welcomed the response.

I stand in the Presence of the Most High with my charge ever before me.

In the depths of my soul, I take off my shoes and then erect, barefoot and empty handed, stand on Holy Ground.

The place where I stand is silent and dark, saturated by the Presence of the Thrice Holy One.

Sometimes, the ground gives way beneath my feet and I plummet down to caverns yet unknown to me. There, I may face anew my own shadows or pain, my limitations or my self-absorbed hard-heartedness.

I become increasingly aware of personal broken-ness that keeps me company in my journey. This awareness is not complete, but the willingness and growing courage necessary to become fully aware of my hidden dragons arm me with serenity, courage and dignity.

Still, whenever…however far I fall, I land with the ground of God beneath my feet.

There, in the dazzling unknown and blinding darkness, I summon all my audacity and reach for the One Who IS. He meets me, leads me…and somehow upholds me as I brutally confront my finitude and folly, there in the merciful, infinite depths of the heart of God.

And while I am there, I also turn my gaze toward my charge before me.

I see that we are held together, mysteriously suspended and saturated in the same loving kindness of the Compassionate One.

And, I am spell-bound by my friend's ineffable beauty.

There, in that moment of revelation, I also experience my charge as my brother or sister who wordlessly suffer as they yearn for their true life and their true God. All words fail as we seek our life with the Author of Life.

As my friends face and describe their pain and humility, they do not realize the gift they give me.

They, too, become bearers of the Presence, and as in their incompleteness and need, they mysteriously become vehicles for the presence of God. Their vulnerabilities, even defensiveness…in different ways, offer me a sense of how receptive they are to their own true selves and the Presence of God already within them.

This they show me through the language of the spoken word as well as through the language of the body and soul.

From across the room their presence touches me and I am changed.

It is here, through relationship and Presence, in the silent dialogue of stance (Greek: *proseuche*), where I the therapist endeavor to be authentic with these cherished, loved ones.

It is standing in the Presence of the Most High *and* with my friends where I can be free to respond with authenticity.

Authenticity here, also takes on its ancient Greek meaning, as this is a kind of authority. It is here in these depths of profound reality, honesty and innocence where opportunities before unseen present themselves and when the dawning of renewal takes place.

It is the Source of this mystery of authentic relationship that ultimately heals, nurtures and transforms us. And, we become evermore unique human persons and our truest selves in the Presence of one another.

Kyriaki Karidoyanes FitzGerald, Ph.D.
October 1999, January 2005.
All rights reserved.

II

Looking Toward the Future:

The Ministries of Women

Looking Toward the Future: The Ministries of Women

Introduction: The Call to the Holiness of God

In the previous presentations, I outlined basic concerns related to authentic relationships. How we view ourselves, the way we relate to one another as Christians and the manner by which we structure our Church, are all meant to reflect the reality of God. For Orthodox Christians, the Trinitarian God is the "ultimate paradigm of human relations." This is because human persons are created in the "image and likeness" (Gen. 1:26) of this same Trinitarian God. We, too, in a creaturely manner, are invited to participate in this same vocation for authentic relationships. We, too, are called to grow in communion with God and each other in ways that express receptive, loving surrender. In creation, the prototype for loving surrender is the incarnation and mission of our Lord, Jesus Christ.

The ancient adage made popular by St. Athanasius from the fourth century, "God became a human person so that the human person may become divine,"[1] identifies our fundamental vocation as sons and daughters of God. How this may take place for each of us usually involves a life-long process. It entails our persistent, fundamental and radical personal honesty to discern and respond to the will of God in our lives, moment by moment. As we faithfully endeavor to "hear the word of God and act on it" (Lk. 8:21), we will find ourselves experiencing countless opportunities that invite us to realize once again the will of God for those persons with whom we are in relationship and the environment in which we find ourselves. In the final analysis, the essential concern of authentic relationships is not "all about us," it is rather about our response to the merciful triune God who loved us first!

This foundation has profound ramifications in how we may engage other human persons. There are no ironclad assumptions we can make regarding our relationship with other people. Jumping to conclusions about others implies that "it is all about us" rather than our grateful response to the merciful God who loves us first. Whenever we make assumptions about other people, we run the risk of "playing God" by projecting our interpretation of reality onto the person with whom we are supposed to be "relating."

People may or may not elect to cooperate in a less than genuine relationship. On the one hand, if persons choose to "play along" voluntarily, we may have reason to wonder from what kind of personal gain each party involved believes he or she may be benefiting as a result of these interactions. This dynamic points to a certain kind of spiritual (as well as psychological) disorder. If, on the other hand, "playing along" occurs less willingly, perhaps out of a desire to please and/or out of fear, these relationships may reflect other types of spiritual (as well as psychological) disorder.

In either case, little genuine growth toward our authentic vocation occurs in these dynamics. Sadly, when it comes to discerning the ministries of women in the Church, there is often much similar projection occurring within various circles of discussion regarding what "women should do." It is far less common to hear deeper, more penetrating questions, such as, "how could God be calling (men and) women to serve Him, today?" Even more particularly, "how could the Lord be calling my daughter, my friend, my colleague, my sister, my wife or me to serve Him, today?"

The very process of asking and valuing these types of questions affects us spiritually. By humbly asking these important questions, our answers may present themselves in time. By honestly struggling with these questions, we also summon the courage and strength to place aside our personal, fallen ego-based preconceptions and remain alert to discerning the will of God for the person and situation at hand (as well as for our own selves). This is not as easy as it may sound. This effort actually involves ongoing, strenuous discipline. With the help of the merciful God, we endeavor to discern the genuinely holy in our lives and respond to it in spirit and in truth.

This demanding effort is a fundamental aspect of Orthodox Christian spiritual discipline. As on a creaturely level, each one of us is invited to become holy as God Himself is Holy (*aghios*). Another way to express this is that we are all called to become "saints," holy ones of God, "participants of divine nature (cf. 2 Pet. 1:4, cf. 1 Pet 2:5,9). It is important not to overlook the fact that the scriptural English translation of "holy" and "saint" derive from the same biblical Greek word, *aghios*. As impossible as this appears, human persons are called to share in the very holiness of God. We become holy only as we exercise the gift of our free will and become ever more receptive to the will and love of God for us, progressing in genuine relationship with Him, ourselves, others and creation.

Even if we were to conduct a cursory review of Church history and the lives of the saints, we would soon realize that there certainly is a "cloud of witnesses" (Heb. 12:1) who have been bearing witness to Christ through the work of the Holy Spirit in a myriad of ways. Reflecting their differing historical contexts and unique circumstances, these men and women grew in authentic relationship with God, themselves, others and creation. Each in their own unique manner became personal vehicles for the presence of the loving God to make Himself known. Even as we appreciated historical similarities and differences and sociocultural influences in the transcription of their lives, we would still come to the same general conclusion that there is no simplistic "cookie-cutter" definition of what a saint looks like. This is founded in the reality that every human person is an intentional, unique and unrepeatable creation of the love of the living God.

Throughout history, women have responded to the love of God in countless ways. They have responded continuously to Christ's invitation to follow Him and to successfully "run the race" (Heb. 12:1) from the first days of His earthly ministry. Indeed, the vast majority of women have grown in holiness by following the Lord courageously through the seemingly unending daily responsibilities and trials their relationships with family members, husbands, children, friends and associates bring. Their personal and collective witness serves as part of the living and vibrant human bedrock upon which the Church stands.

Present Concerns

It is the legacy of women following Christ in publicly visible and dynamic ways which particularly concerns me when considering the future of women's ministries from within the limits of this discussion. In my investigation of the ordination of women deacons,[2] I began by calling attention to the witness of a number of female saints from the apostolic era. Later on, a number of other women who lived in different centuries and are remembered in the calendar of the Orthodox Church as saints are also reviewed. Even under some of the direst historical circumstances (e.g., persecutions, wars, the Crusades, Muslim conquests, World Wars, the rise and fall of Communism, etc.,), we would soon discern that a number of holy women followed Christ in visible and dynamic ways, including through expressions of pastoral, evangelical and/or apostolic leadership.

For this discussion, I am using these three terms with a specific and essential understanding as a starting point. These terms point to three profoundly interrelated and observable phenomena from within the lives of the saints through the centuries. By "pastoral," I am referring to expressions of ministry that "shepherd" others' journey in Christ in some manner. The flock to be guided may be a family, a parish or a monastic community. The flock could also include spiritual sons and daughters who present themselves privately to their spiritual mother or spiritual father for direction in the conduct of their lives. By "evangelical," I am referring to expressions of ministry that in some way "share the good news" with others. This effort may take place within a small community of sisters and/or brothers, or be expressed by a mission on a much larger scale. And, by "apostolic," I am referring to those who have been "sent out" to establish and build the Church in a particular time and place.

The legacy of women following Christ in these ways concerns me when considering the future of women's ministries. The

Church throughout history is obliged to the loving God, the "Giver of gifts," to discern, test, receive and support the vocations of the many holy women who were called to follow Him from within the various contexts of their lives. Of course, this is just as true for male followers of the Lord.

The lives of the saints bear witness to the fact that throughout history many women have responded to Christ in ways that included expressions of service that became more visible and dynamic. For over half a century, numerous thoughtful Orthodox have noticed that much has been said to affirm this truth, yet too little has been done to discern, test, receive and support the various ways women today are being called particularly to these above-mentioned expressions of ministry. Even certain structures within the Church that in the past included the leadership of women are hard pressed to be seen today.

A Pain-filled Compromised Witness

Whenever I am invited to teach or speak across North America and elsewhere around the world, I am often cautiously approached by a number of devoted and sensitive women who desire to serve God beyond the ministries they have customarily seen in their local communities. Most of these persons share a deep, ongoing hope to serve the Church through some expression of life-long vocational lay ministry. Their interests generally reflect the pastoral, evangelical and/or apostolic dimensions described above. These women frequently relate disturbing stories of their endeavor to cultivate a deeper expression of service that is being ignored, minimized or undermined by persons "who should know better." Some from among this number confided with perhaps additional trepidation that they have experienced a "call" to ordained ministry and sought out persons in authority for direction and assistance in order to facilitate the next appropriate step. They too, all too often, left gravely disappointed.

To a degree that weighs inexplicably heavily on the soul, every one of these women have been profoundly hurt and disheartened. In their ongoing effort to honor their call, most of them to some degree were forced to bear the painful cross of invisibility imposed by certain members of the Church. A number of these women have suffered for many years, some for several decades. A few, it must be acknowledged, have left the Church in despair both for themselves and for us. Nevertheless, it appears that the majority of these women remain faithful.

Many questions begin springing to mind here. Recognizing our call to authentic relationships, we must ask the following:

> • How authentic are relationships when the presence and will of God for a person is not recognized, received and cultivated?
> • How much worse is it when a genuine call is discounted, ignored or even treated with contempt?
> • What does this say about those who should know better?
> • What does this have to say about those persons who privately do recognize these gifts as coming from God, but do nothing to help?
> • How much worse is it for those who intentionally look the other way instead of actively seeking where the Holy Spirit may be leading the people of God?

Our lack of accountability, integrity and courage to respond to how God may be working among all His people backfires; and this crippling inertia severely compromises the quality of our own witness! St. Paul reminds us, "When one member suffers, all suffer together" (1 Cor. 12:26). Whenever Christians ignore, minimize, intimidate or oppress other followers –female or male - who are striving to respond with humility and courage to a genuine call from God, a grievous sin is being committed. And this is blasphemy of the Holy Spirit.

Displaced Fears of Women in Ministry

As members of the Church, we must carefully proceed on this matter in a way that shows concern for authentic relationships but at the same time shows concern for the Church. It must be stressed here that from an Orthodox perspective, this two-fold concern is not a contradiction. Rather, it reflects our unconditional accountability to the love of the living God. We are bound, first of all, to reach out to the God who loved us first in humility and prayer, seeking to discern His will through the gracious action of the Holy Spirit for the present situation being considered.

In recent years, great fear has been expressed by a relatively small but vocal number from within the Orthodox community that a secular, political feminist agenda will infiltrate the Orthodox Church regarding the ministries of women if we "allow" our women to minister in more visible and dynamic ways.

In point of fact, this type of fear may possibly indicate a polarizing, sectarian perspective which is "infiltrating" the life of the Church. One wonders if this negativity toward women in ministry may reflect the fears of a few Orthodox relative neophytes who left their previous faith communities partly because of the secular politicizing of various issues including women's ministries. Others who promote this negativity may have an unexamined, legalistic definition of the Church and Tradition. In most cases, it appears that for some reason the breadth and depth of this topic has not been fully engaged from the perspective of living Orthodox Tradition.

We must bear in mind here that any political ideology, including a feminist one, when approached as an end in itself, becomes a kind of ersatz religion. And like every false religion, a politically based, ersatz religion essentially defines reality from the perspective of fallen human-based interpretations of power instead of accountability before the living God. Women endeavoring to serve God in "spirit and in truth" (Jn. 4:24) seek to respond to the call of Jesus Christ not the call of an ersatz religion. And hopefully, much in the same manner God-loving men strive to discern the Lord's will for themselves in their life and work. God-loving women seeking to do the same would place their relationship with God above everything else including any kind of political ideology or agenda.

Today, a small, but vocal number appear to be seeking control over the vocations of women by severely limiting their expression. Sometimes a heavy-handed attack is wielded rather than seeking with sensitivity to discern the will of God in each of these cases. Verses from Scripture and examples from Tradition are cited, frequently out of context, in order to justify loveless assumptions, projections and behaviors. In some circumstances, these actions seem to personify the popular one line joke: "don't confuse me with the truth, because I've already made up my mind!"

Sadly, it seems as if there are persons who are not interested in knowing how God may be calling women today, and as a consequence, men as well! For this limited number, the effort to restrict cavalierly, the ministries of women may in the final analysis, have little to do with the love of God. Ironically, these attitudes and behaviors demonstrate most, if not all, of the characteristics of a human self-serving, power-oriented agenda-driven ideology.

Three Spiritual Failures

There are at least three other simultaneous spiritual wrongs that are being promoted here. First, there is a gross failure of desire in seeking to discern where God may be leading each of these female persons, today. What is even more tragic, this type of failure reflects a gross hardness of heart reflected in the soul of the perpetrator because "where your treasure is, there your heart lies, also" (Mt. 6:21). How faithful can the perpetrator be to his or her true vocation from God under such circumstances?

Second, this lack of desire reflects a personal resistance to where God is leading his Church for our times. A gross failure of seeking to discern the "signs of the times" (Mt. 16:3) reflects an unwillingness and inability to perceive the presence and will of Christ within the present context. Orthodox spiritual tradition affirms that the presence and will of God must be sought courageously with every "sign" set before us, be it experienced as a blessing or as a catastrophe.

Third, by creating and operating out of a false image of the Church and our place in it, we set ourselves up for future disasters.

This is because our actions do not manifest the will of the living God of love; instead, they promote a delusion. While throughout history, bad times and disasters sometimes occur outside human control as believers we must avoid compounding their damage. Yet, how easily we can increase the severity of calamities as well as sow the seeds for new ones whenever we operate out of complacency, pretexts and false premises.

These failings all reflect profound spiritual disease. Through these wrongs, human beings in effect, are telling God how to act in creation, how to attend to His flock, even how to call his servants! Each of these failings displays an astounding lack of humility. As usual, the Christian response to those who define the church essentially in polarizing, political and/or self-absorbed terms comes from outside these life-effacing extremes. The Church's response is one based in "spirit and in truth" (Jn. 4:24).

Toward a Spiritual Response: Orthodox Women Discern

We may begin to gain insight on how to respond from Orthodox women themselves. I will do this by reflecting upon two important conferences. First, I will reflect upon the process, how I have witnessed Orthodox women working and discerning together. Second, I will relate some of the content of what these persons as members of the Church discern to be important regarding the future of women's ministries. The source of these observations comes from two international Orthodox women's conferences that were organized in the 1990's on behalf of the Orthodox churches.

Orthodox women, indeed, have been reflecting upon the ministry of the Church and other vital issues that affect them. One of the greatest privileges of my life was the invitation extended to me by the Orthodox churches to design and facilitate two international conferences for Orthodox women and about Orthodox women. These were organized and implemented through the offices of the World Council of Churches (WCC). A common theme was chosen for these two meetings: "Discerning the 'Signs of the Times' (Matt. 16:3): Women in the Life of the Orthodox Church." Our intention was to strive to offer "a singular event in two different contexts." The first conference was held in Damascus, Syria during 4-10 October 1996. This brought together women representing the Orthodox churches in Asia, Africa and the Middle East. Our host was His Beatitude Patriarch Ignatios IV, Greek Orthodox Patriarch of Antioch and All the East. There were over sixty-five participants who attended this Conference.

The second international conference took place in Istanbul (Constantinople), Turkey during 10-17 May 1997. This meeting brought together Orthodox women representing churches from North and South America, Eastern and Western Europe, and Russia. Ecumenical Patriarch Bartholomew of Constantinople hosted this second conference. There were over fifty persons who attended this meeting.

The theme for these Conferences actually originated about six months before the meeting in Damascus. During the second week of December 1995, on the occasion of his first official visit to the WCC, Ecumenical Patriarch Bartholomew was invited to participate in a news conference. One of the interviewers invited His All-holiness to discuss the possibility of the rejuvenation of the ministry of women deacons. After displaying openness to the possibility, he concluded the interview by stating:

> It is important to watch for 'the signs of the times' (Mt. 16:3) and to fine-tune our ears to the stirring and calls of the Spirit as recommended in the Apocalypse, 'he who has an ear, let him hear what the Spirit says to the Churches' (Rev. 2:7).[3]

Apparently, the Ecumenical Patriarch believes that the ministry of women is an important issue that well deserves "discerning" during our present "times." He also does this by plainly identifying the source and greater context of this process. This effort does not originate with fallible male or female human persons, central as they may be, but rather, with the "calls of the Spirit...'he who has an ear, let him hear...'"[4]

The common goal uniting these conferences was for the Church to hear the concerns of Orthodox women from around the world on issues that were most important to them. It is important to note that the great majority of those who came were formally appointed as delegates. They were appointed by their presiding hierarchs who were themselves acting on behalf of their regional synods. The delegates were responsible for officially representing the concerns of Orthodox women from their regional churches. There was also a smaller number of other supportive persons in attendance. They generously served as hosts, consultants, presenters, and local contributors.

None of the organizers were certain who or what kind of person the churches would send to these meetings. To be sure, we anticipated a wide range of possibilities: women of various racial and ethnic backgrounds, ages, social, economic and educational backgrounds, married women, mothers, single women, wives of priests, nuns, abbesses, theologians, educators, parish, diocese and archdiocese administrators, civil servants, students, professors, university administrators, diplomats and political leaders, medical doctors and nurses, not the least of whom would be women deeply involved with local, regional or international philanthropy. We also anticipated a wide range of theological and spiritual maturity. Some would know about Orthodoxy only through their local experience and others would have studied Orthodox life and theology extensively.

Thankfully, we anticipated this wide variety of persons possibly coming, and it was precisely this range that was appointed to come. Through divine intervention and the hard work of the delegates and other participants, these meetings proved to be a great success as they produced an unexpected and history-making "gift." For the first time in history we can now say – at least on a preliminary level – a global consensus on important issues that concern Orthodox women has been achieved from the perspective of Orthodox women. The two official statements of the conferences as well as the majority of the papers presented to the delegates have been published in *Orthodox Women Speak: Discerning the 'Signs of the Times.'*[5]

Discerning from a Spiritual Foundation

I will share with you here some of the most important spiritual lessons these women taught me. These meetings became unexpectedly a school for authentic relationships. As mentioned earlier, while diverse, these women were united by their common faith in Christ. Despite sometimes very difficult circumstances, they naturally identified themselves as full members of the Church. This may surprise those who believe that Orthodox women are "second class" citizens. In fact, the most striking and virtually universal spiritual quality I noticed among these women was their profound and graceful ease with themselves as Orthodox Christians. They identified themselves fully with the Church even as they had to face very difficult regional circumstances. It is important to bear in mind here that most of the representatives were in the process of experiencing, or had recently experienced some form of long-term political and/or socio-economic hardship.

Many delegates represented constituencies where Orthodox Christians, and even all Christians generally, are in the minority. Others came from countries that were riddled with poverty and/or widespread famine. Still others came from places where Christians are actively persecuted. Many were trying to rebuild both their local congregations and communities after years of war, oppressive political regimes or civil strife. Despite all of these difficulties, these diverse Orthodox women arrived at the meetings with the belief that they came to serve the Church.

On Spiritual Discernment

Perhaps as a consequence of this positive, spiritual foundation, there appeared to be three additional spiritual, and yet concrete qualities they held in common, despite their numerous and apparent differences. These qualities felt virtually palpable. Perhaps that was due to these specific qualities which in the end were in the service of the gift of discernment. A gift that allowed the fruit of global consensus on major issues that concern Orthodox women to become known. And these qualities are the following: thankfulness, generosity and hospitality.

At this point, it is important to identify the importance of discernment within Orthodox Christian spiritual tradition. Orthodox theological and spiritual tradition teaches that discernment is one of the highest gifts bestowed to the believer by the Holy Spirit of God. Discernment essentially is that capacity granted through the activity of the Holy Spirit to perceive and engage the truth in each situation while abiding in the presence of the love of the living God despite potentially dangerous distractions. One's "heart," in other words, (or one's entire being) is ready to receive and implement to the best of his or her ability what is discerned as God's will for the given situation.

Believers are to strive continuously to seek and cultivate this gift. They do this by first endeavoring to grow in the virtue of "purity of heart" before God. Purity of heart may be briefly identified here as the discipline of being able to "hear the word of God and do it" (Lk. 8:21) from the depth of one's being. This endeavor requires profound courage as it ceaselessly urges us to examine our own conscience, motives and behaviors in the presence of God, and then follow through with congruent action.

Truly, we can never succeed in attaining the gift of discernment alone. We rely on the loving God's forgiveness and mercy in order to have this gift come to fruition. Along with the psalmist we, too, cry: "Create in me a pure heart, O God; and renew a right spirit within me (Ps. 50:10)." As this foundation is established and matures with God's help, one begins to enjoy the fruit of growing in relationship with God as well with as one's own self, others and creation. Discernment is arguably the most important quality after which the ancient Church sought for its leadership, particularly in Her bishops.

On Thankfulness

The delegates taught through their example that persons growing in discernment also exemplify a number of spiritual, yet concrete qualities, including thankfulness, generosity, and hospitality. The first quality, thankfulness, was very difficult for me, as an Orthodox Christian from North America, to appreciate. As so many of these women were survivors of difficult contexts, why were they so cheerful? Why were they so kind? In all of my previous international assignments, I had never met so many patient people in the same context as I had meeting these women.

We can easily give a simplistic answer, and say that they were "grateful" for the privilege of representing their churches, or for being granted a reprieve from their difficult circumstances. But they showed only joy in returning home after our meeting, as well. They exuded an "attitude of gratitude" which transcended their difficult circumstances.

What I learned from them is that their gratitude is based in the fact that God first loved us. He loved us even before we could or would choose to love Him. His unconditional love for us does not depend upon our love for Him. Somehow, in the various difficulties they had to face, they discovered that nothing can take us away from the love of God. And so, evil does not have to be met with evil. Crime does not have to be reciprocated by crime. They generally were not resentful, nor cynical, despite enormous challenges for some. Instead, they were receptive to new people, new ideas and new ways that the love of God could make itself present. Collectively, they were cheerful, peaceful and very attentive. Simultaneously, they demonstrated a deep kind of maturity and innocence.

This foundation made our dialogue very fruitful. In fact, I have found that this quality of compassionate, focused attention has been too rare a commodity in professional theological and ecumenical settings – Orthodox and non-Orthodox alike! The acceptance, serenity and gratitude expressive of the conviction "that God loves us first" demonstrated by these women, in my mind at least, made the difference in both of the conferences.

This very powerful "attitude of gratitude," so to speak, results only from a disciplined surrender to God. Surrender, the ability to let go of our finite and self-centered conceptions of what is "mine," releases us spiritually and psychologically. Surrender enables us to ask God and others for help. The ability to be thankful, truly, is a fruit of surrender. Surrender allows us to receive the love of God to the depths of our soul and makes us receptive to seeing life on His terms. Surrender also demands the courage required for us to be more open and honest in discerning what godly and fallen influences reside in our own depths.

When an "attitude of gratitude" is feigned from a frozen heart, what we will have is a kind of inauthentic, double life…one frozen reality on the inside, and another on the outside. Eventually, this wreaks havoc in our own lives and in the lives we touch. The women who were appointed by their hierarchs to come to these important conferences could not have recognized the other foreign Orthodox women as sisters if they were not already receptive in their hearts and minds to the love of the living God.

On Generosity

The second quality, generosity, was actually the most visibly dominant quality that I noticed about them. My fear was that they would be generous "to a fault" with their time, goods and energies toward us, and thus perhaps even compromising their own participation in our deliberations in some way. This, however, did not happen.

Perhaps my unfounded fears were based on my experience of our own North American and western society. Our society today increasingly places more and more attention on status, power, material wealth and the obtaining of goods…the neverending pursuit of *things*. This of course, reflects a distorted relationship with God's world. While wealth and material goods are gifts from God to us, it is very easy to confuse the gifts for the Giver of the gifts. The more we confuse one for the other, the less easily we see opportunities around us to do good. For too many of us, it seems as if the more we have in the nature of material success, the less need we see around us. We then respond less and less generously, for where our hearts lie, there we find our treasures also (cf. Mt. 6:21).

While living in Switzerland in the 1990's, my husband and I had the honor of meeting the famous Orthodox nun, Mother Sophia, and a number of her closest associates. Even though she was living in Lausanne, arguably the wealthiest city in Switzerland at the time, a city that was located in one of the wealthiest countries in the world, she began a ministry to the forgotten and the destitute. In the beginning, she received much criticism for her work, as the majority of the locals believed that she was wasting her time. They saw no need for her work in the affluent city of Lausanne. Nevertheless, Mother Sophia began a campaign to minister to drug and alcohol addicts, street persons, those infected with HIV and AIDS, unwed mothers and the homeless. Even in the most beautiful and prosperous city of Lausanne, she found hundreds of persons in need who benefited from her assistance.

Within a few short years, Mother Sophia had become the most revered religious figure in all of Switzerland, second only to Mother Teresa! She certainly had her detractors, as she was a controversial survivor of her own tragic and painful psychiatric history. Nevertheless, no one could fault her for her stewardship![6] She was highly respected for spending huge sums of money towards these ministries, very wisely. Not unlike the example set before us by Mother Sophia, generosity helps us remain centered upon the Giver of the gifts so as to be able to wisely respond to the needs around us.

On Hospitality

The third quality is hospitality. Orthodox women (and men) are famous for their hospitality in many parts of the world. While this is wonderful in and of itself, there is a deeper significance to the virtue of hospitality. Genuine hospitality demonstrates in concrete terms a willingness to reach out and receive the stranger – "the other."

Whenever we open ourselves enough to receive another, we also potentially let go of our own personal *status quo*. We offer intimate aspects of our life that are of value to ourselves, and we receive something, someone new, even strange. Every expression of authentic hospitality involves risk. In the Old Testament, we read of Abraham and his wife, Sarah, warmly receiving and entertaining three strange visitors under their tent (Gen 18). The story reveals to us that the strangers lavishly welcomed into the home of Abraham and Sarah were actually divine messengers, angels sent by God. And as we know from the story, Abraham and Sarah themselves, were changed, as a result of this visitation.

In the New Testament, we read about another striking event concerning hospitality. In this story (Lk 24:13-35), we see two of Jesus' disciples walking the seven mile journey from Jerusalem to Emmaus. It was the third day after the crucifixion and death of the Lord. As they walk, they encounter a stranger who was going in the same direction as they. The stranger meets them just as they are in the depths of their sadness and discussing the terrible events that had occurred in the past three days. The stranger asks them what had happened, and they replied to the stranger with frankness: "Are you the only stranger in Jerusalem who does not know the things that have taken place there during these days?" And the stranger replies: "What things?"

This marks the beginning of a profound encounter as the two disciples share with this stranger the whole story of who Jesus was and how he was condemned to death by crucifixion. "Now" they tell him, "Now on the third day since these things took place. . . some women of our group have astounded us." And the two proceeded to tell the stranger how the women disciples had been to the tomb, found it empty and were told by angels that Jesus had risen.

At this point, the encounter with this stranger takes an unpredictable turn He – the stranger – takes the lead and says to them, "Oh, how foolish you are, and how slow of heart to believe all that the prophets have declared! Was it not necessary for the Messiah to have suffered these things and then enter into His glory?" The stranger now spends the rest of the journey instructing them about the Messiah beginning with Moses and the prophets.

Most of you probably remember this story and recall that it does not end here. The three reach the town of Emmaus. The stranger appears to be continuing his journey. On seeing this, the disciples invite him to have dinner and stay with them for the night as it was already almost evening. It was only when the three sat down to break bread and eat together when the true identity of the stranger was revealed to the two disciples. It was the Risen Lord, Jesus Himself!

Welcoming the stranger remains an important custom in Orthodox family life today. In fact, it is more than a custom: it is a necessary discipline that is expressive of Christian life. We must recall here that the Greek word for visitor and stranger is the same: *xenos*. I remember during special days of celebration, but especially feast days like Pascha (Easter), Christmas, New Year's, Name Day celebrations, even on Thanksgiving, my mother or grandmother would set an extra place at the table. I was told, "we set the extra place at our table for the unexpected visitor…because that person could be an angel or Christ, Himself coming to visit us in disguise."

Hospitality was reflected in another custom and this concerns how the *Vasilopita* (St. Basil's New Year's Bread) was to be cut. One of the first pieces to be cut in my family, just after the pieces cut in honor of our Lord and His mother, was the slice that honored the *xenos*. And the first visitor who crossed the threshold of our home after the cutting of the *Vasilopita*, was given this slice of honor. Here, even in the most personal and private family scenes, room was made to welcome the stranger, the 'other.'

In our own parishes, we must be ready to set a place at the table for the visitors and strangers who come to us even if they are very different from us. It is important to practice the loving discipline of hospitality toward the various kinds of people who may come to our churches. The women delegates who were sent by the churches in numerous ways embodied this discipline. They came to recognize and joyfully welcome one another as sisters in the faith. Otherwise, they would not have been able too discuss so openly the numerous sensitive challenges which presented themselves during our deliberations; nor would they have been so receptive in examining the various ministries that are necessary for the Church, both for the present and future.

It was profoundly apparent to me that from the depths of their hearts these Orthodox women received one another as sisters. Many observed how this realization was virtually tangible as it energized the delegates to focus even more attentively on each other's concerns. On a deeply spiritual level, we may appreciate this as a fruit of the receptive hospitality they gave to each other in the presence of God.

Sophrosyne

If I could take thankfulness, generosity, and hospitality to try and learn what these words may be teaching us, I would say that these taken together point to the virtue known in Greek as *sophrosyne*. This is a wonderful word and there is no literal translation for it in English. *Sophrosyne* is loosely translated into English as prudence, discretion, chastity, moderation, faithfulness in marriage, and even sobriety.

This is a difficult word to translate as it suggests both a wholeness of life as well as a demonstrated depth of wisdom. *Sophrosyne* is expressed through personal integrity in the presence of God within the context of one's daily experiences. The person who is a bearer of *sophrosyne* whether he or she knows it or not somehow tends to leave a situation better than she or he found it. This may be due to the fact that the one who emanates this virtue is essentially concerned with the salvation of all those with whom she or he may come into contact.

This was an important quality sought after by the ancient church when communities were seeking to elect leaders to shepherd them: be they men called to serve through the episcopacy and presbyterate, or men and women called to serve through the diaconate. As Christian monasticism developed through the centuries, sophrosyne was sought out from among the candidates during the election process of a community's spiritual father (abbot) or spiritual mother (abbess). Christians of the early Church diligently aspired in their spiritual lives toward acquiring sophrosyne. Sophrosyne is another essential characteristic that is a consequence of living in an authentic relationship with God, others, the cosmos and even, oneself.[7]

"Speaking the Truth in Love"

In hindsight, I can attest that it was perhaps the virtue of *sophrosyne* that guided the priorities and actions of the majority of the women present. This is because the concern for the salvation of Christ was the common thread that weaved itself throughout our proceedings. There were a number of important issues discussed at these meetings most of which cannot be repeated here due to lack of space, but may be found in the statements and papers delivered to the delegates.

Nevertheless, some of these concerns deserve to be repeated here as they identify the essential focus of our topic. Their findings discuss the present status of women in the Orthodox Church, the many ways Orthodox women are presently serving the Church throughout the world and the call of attention to important concerns for future ministries. In particular, how this information is being "received" by the greater Church has a direct bearing upon our present concern for authentic relationships.

As mentioned earlier, both documents reflect the assumption that the delegates regard themselves as full members of the Church. There is even an apparent ease and comfort displayed with their identity as Orthodox women. This manner of taking their membership in the Church for granted, however, also established a deep sense of accountability among the participants "to speak the truth in love" (Eph. 4:15) to each other both during formal and informal discussions.

This deep sense of accountability to each other in the presence of God also compelled them to call attention to certain practices in the Church that compromise the Gospel and impede the mission and witness of the Church. This includes calling attention to abuses and sins that affect the status and participation of women in the life of the Church. The ramifications of sexism as a sin was discussed at both Conferences. The text from the Damascus Conference, for example, states:

> We note with tremendous sadness, how easily it is for the presence of women to be forgotten.... There

are some occasions when the role and presence of women, as well as their work, is not always validated for the value it has… Rather, women may be seen by some as more readily dispensable.

The text continues, furthermore, by stating:

> Women have also been dismissed in other ways as well. We recognize with deep concern how social injustices such as poverty, illiteracy and invisibility may effect Orthodox women and women in general, in our part of the world. Wherever possible, we must strive to assist them and open our lives and our hearts to them, as our Lord would have us do.

The Istanbul text takes this a step further. The delegates suggest that sexism as a topic be engaged in various ways programmatically by the Church. They recommend that:

> The issue of sexism be seriously considered. The Church would benefit from theological and soteriological reflection on this issue especially through the medium of consultations, workshops and informal study.

A similar focus was echoed almost ten years prior in the Statement from the 1988 Rhodes, Greece Inter-Orthodox Consultation on the Place of Women in the Orthodox Church. This Consultation emphasized the necessity of needing to:

> Confess in honesty and humility that, owing to human weakness and sinfulness, the Christian communities have not always and in all places been able to suppress effectively ideas, manners and customs, historical developments and social conditions which have resulted in practical discrimination against women. Human sinfulness

has thus led to practices which do not reflect the true nature of the Church of Jesus Christ.[8]

Both the Damascus and Istanbul discussions and documents, furthermore, expressed concern regarding certain liturgical practices associated with the presentation of infants, particular prayers related to miscarriage, post-partum mothers, and the assumptions which in some places prohibited women from receiving communion for biological reasons. These concerns were openly, yet with great sensitivity, discussed by the participants. The delegates recognized the need to more thoughtfully examine the present relationship between theology and praxis. The focus upon *orthopraxia* as the theologically correct application of practice was indeed at the heart of each Conference's discussions.

The Istanbul meeting, for example, clearly stated that a number of practices "do not properly express the theology of the church regarding the dignity of God's creation of women and her redemption in Jesus Christ." This was in part, a thoughtful reflection to the concern expressed by the Damascus delegates that there are, "certain liturgical practices which need immediate attention as we believe they do indeed, diminish the dignity of women."

Apparently, these concerns have begun to be taken more seriously as demonstrated through the courageous and thoughtful actions by a number of Orthodox leaders. The Synod of the Greek Orthodox Patriarchate of Antioch, under the leadership of His Beatitude, Patriarch Ignatius IV, immediately responded to these very concerns raised by the Damascus Conference. These same themes were also identified a few weeks earlier during the month of August by a regional meeting of Orthodox women from the Middle East. "The Synod affirmed the God-given value of women in the Church and ordered that liturgical texts which imply otherwise be corrected." Furthermore,

> The Holy Synod discussed certain matters which touched the lives of women and decided that women and men should be treated equally con-

cerning their participation in divine services and receiving sacraments. Whatever references are in the liturgical books that women are unclean and tainted should be corrected...This necessitates a new look at liturgical texts.[9]

At long last, these latest decisions finally began to implement the earlier recommendation from the 1988 Rhodes Consultation:

> [The Orthodox] are bound to affirm in the strongest possible way the dignity of the human person, both the female and the male. Any act which denies the dignity of the human person and any act which discriminates against women and men on the basis of gender is a sin. It is therefore the task of the Church to affirm before the world the dignity of the human person, created in the image and likeness of God (Gen. 1:26).[10]

Frustration with the "Circular File"

Following the Rhodes Conference, little action was taken. The apparent lack of enthusiasm and commitment by Church leaders to apply the *orthopraxia* previously advised at Rhodes and elsewhere was glaring. This inaction was experienced as a source of frustration and even embarrassment by the vast majority in attendance at both conferences. A humorous irritation toward the "circular file" (i.e., the trash can) was raised repeatedly by a number of delegates. In hindsight, we may consider this type of inaction as an expression of in-authentic relationships. This is due to the fact that the sincere concerns of faithful members of the Church that have been repeated over decades still remain unaddressed. The Istanbul text stresses that:

> Many recommendations have emerged from previous meetings of Orthodox women. While some recommendations have been addressed others have not. We are concerned about the reception

of this document and recommend our churches make this statement available for women either through general publications or correspondence to parishes.[11]

With a special note of concern for expanding the scope of ministries for women, the Damascus meeting similarly emphasizes "that we still wait for the application of the recommendations from the 1988 Inter-Orthodox Rhodes Consultation on "The Place of Woman in the Orthodox Church."

Discerning the Ministries of Women from a Spiritual Foundation

Perhaps due in part to these above concerns, the participants at both meetings through their actions collectively bore witness to the mature spiritual foundation required for discerning every ministry. This foundation serves to deepen one's relationship with Christ and others in a manner that facilitates authentic relationships. Orthodox spirituality generally prioritizes every action we take from the perspective of the Lord's essential commandment: "you shall love the Lord, your God with all your heart, soul and mind….and…your neighbor as yourself" (Mt. 22:37-39). This commandment is stated more succinctly with this similar directive, "seek first His Kingdom and His righteousness, and all else will be added to you, as well" (Mt. 6:33). In order to keep these priorities straight, human based definitions of authority, position and power are not to have the final say. Here, we may recall Jesus' clear admonition: "What does it profit a person to gain the whole world and lose one's own soul?" (Mt. 16:26).

With this in mind and emphasizing the recommendations of previous meetings, both Conferences stressed the importance of the role of the laity within the Church. It became clear quickly to the participants that the practices of the various Orthodox communities varied widely on this issue. In some places, laymen and laywomen are actively involved in various expressions of ministry virtually in an analogous manner. This included positions of leadership and influence in the life of the Church. In a number of other places, this was clearly not the case. The Istanbul delegates stated, "women are able to and should be invited to offer guidance to the Church on issues that specifically concern them." The Damascus representatives recommended "that our leaders encourage women's involvement and participation in the every day decision-making process of our local churches."

Bearing in mind the spiritual foundation of this process, the women delegates discerned that they, too, had to act. The delegates in Istanbul demonstrated a strong commitment "to stimulate a desire in our people to take an active role in the life of the Church. This may happen with the realization, on the part of Orthodox Christians, of their own royal priesthood." While it was acknowledged that much is required of Orthodox leadership to support this undertaking, many participants at this meeting committed themselves, personally, to educate the laity more assertively regarding the various ministries fitting for the royal priesthood.

This fresh expression of enthusiasm and commitment to reach out to other members of the laity must be commended and supported! This commitment to action affirms the truth of the ancient spiritual insight that even "the least person can make the greatest difference." Speaking about this very same principle to participants attending a seminar on the "Environment and Religious Education" during the Feast of the Holy Spirit (June 1994), Ecumenical Patriarch Bartholomew of Constantinople confesses:

> Permit us to confide our thoughts to you: *We do not place much trust in the strong and the mighty, or in people of authority. We believe, rather, in those willing and patient individuals, in those who do not lose sight of their objective*, namely the objective of the good. Do not forget the acknowledgement of the ancient Greeks that "drops of water can make even rocks hollow." Many simple people, in various small corners of the earth, with nominal but continuous daily concerns, are able to change the world, even if only slightly, for the better. Today, on the day after Pentecost, we celebrate the Feast

of the Holy Spirit. We celebrate the triumph of the few, the weak – at least by human standards – holy disciples and apostles of our Lord, who, empowered by the fire of Pentecost changed the world some 2,000 years ago, for all time.[12]

Women in Ministry: Today's Challenges and Opportunities

Concerning the many ministries already made visible within the body of Christ, the participants of the Damascus meeting affirmed with gratitude, "we were very happy to learn from each other about the many forms of ministry in which women in our churches are already engaged." Even from among the participants of this meeting:

> We witnessed...some women...were active in monastic life, others were active as single women, wives or mothers, a number were serving within their local parish or diocese, other participants were active in the ecumenical movement, some were involved with the study or teaching of theology, and many were involved in philanthropic, medical and/or educational service in association either with the Church, or a respected regional or national institution.

Perhaps as a result of the recent history associated with the fall of the so-called "Iron Curtain," or possibly, reflecting more generally, the present onslaught of challenges raised by contemporary society, a new emphasis was articulated for the concern of lapsed Orthodox. A number of women attending the Istanbul meeting came from areas that had recently experienced the tragedy of war. Delegates touchingly spoke of women as "peacemakers" and called upon the churches to make "a greater commitment to support our sister Orthodox Churches in crisis situations...and to support refugees and those in war-torn situations. Often in these situations, women and children suffer most."

These participants expressed a particularly strong desire for more communication among Orthodox women regarding theological, spiritual and practical concerns that particularly affect them. There was a powerful call for more resources and materials that can be used in the many church schools throughout the Orthodox world. These materials would better assist Christians with living their faith on a daily basis. Some of the delegates from Eastern Europe especially stressed that in addition to receiving food and clothing there is the deeply experienced need to be fed spiritually and theologically. They looked to Orthodox Christians in other parts of the world for assistance.

Women and Orthodox Theological Education

The delegates at both meetings recognized the serious lack of opportunities for women to study Orthodox theology in far too many situations today. The strength of this emphasis was surprising:

> Many women seek deeper knowledge of the Church through theological study. In families and schools, women are the primary educators. Women share this task and learn well from one another. Thus, theologically-educated women have a particular ministry in teaching our faithful. For these reasons, Orthodox theological education for women is a priority and should be facilitated on all levels.

At the Damascus meeting, there was a "deep disappointment" expressed that many women "have not had the chance to study theology in a formal setting such as a seminary or theological school. This hinders our role and work in the Church." This meeting also recommended "that women receive both spiritual and financial support, in order to pursue studies in theological education; relatedly, that more informal opportunities to study and grow in the theology of the Church be created."

There was reported a wide range of experience by those women who had formally studied theology in Orthodox contexts. Some stated that they were appreciated as valued and equal members of their communities. Other women reported suffering rejection and degradation on a daily basis. Sadly, it was quickly realized during the proceedings that the Orthodox generally have not utilized the expertise and experience of their women graduates very well.* The women delegates and consultants who had been fortunate enough to pursue formal studies in Orthodox theology were publicly recognized and encouraged by the rest of the participants at both Conferences.

Both meetings benefited from the blessing of enjoying the participation of monastic women in attendance. The importance of the gift of monasticism to the life of the Church, both historically and today, was frequently appreciated both formally and informally by participants from both meetings. The Istanbul conference stated: "We encourage the development of monastic vocations for women...The very presence of monasticism bears witness to 'the one thing necessary' (Lk. 10:42), to which all are called."

Both meetings expressed a desire for the nurturance and development of ministries in theology, education and mission, ecumenical relations, and pastoral care. Pastoral care seemed to be a particular focus at the Damascus meeting. It was stressed that:

> Our leadership encourages women's formal and informal ministries in pastoral care, so as to reach out to others who may have been spiritually isolated, in material need, grieving the loss of a loved one, survivors of abuse or violence, etc. These persons deserve particular attention, as they require the healing presence and assistance of the Church through Her prayer, counseling and support.

---

* For this reason, St. Catherine's Vision (www.orthodoxwomen.org), a working group comprised mostly of Orthodox theologically informed women dedicated to studying and supporting the many ways women and men are called to serve in the life of the Church today was formed in 2003.

The Ordination of Women

The Conference participants recommended that the churches take more positive actions in affirming and supporting the various vocations to which women may be called. Women in the diaconate was of particular interest at both Conferences. Many examples of women serving the Church actively in a "diaconal" manner were shared by the participants. A number of participants themselves were serving in ministries such as: theological education, spiritual direction, pastoral counseling, Christian education, hospital visitations and medical missions, philanthropy, and caring for orphaned children, the destitute and the elderly in their communities.

Discussions regarding the rejuvenation of women in the diaconate also occurred. The Damascus Conference recognized "the important ministry of deaconesses as a response to the Holy Spirit for various needs of this present age." Furthermore, it was strongly recommended "that our Church leaders discern prayerfully and courageously the presence of the Holy Spirit in those many places where the ministry of ordained deaconesses, as well as other forms of ministry, are needed." The Istanbul delegates stated: "Many of us believe the incorporation of deaconesses in the life of the Church will help contribute to the atmosphere of love and learning, and to the life of the Church." These discussions also revealed that a number of participants were not completely familiar with this tradition of ministry. For these persons, "there is still work to be done in order to come to a fuller understanding" of this ministry.

It became apparent at both meetings that the rejuvenation of the ministry of women deacons has been occurring at perhaps a somewhat faster rate within the Oriental Orthodox family. In the Armenian Orthodox Church of Constantinople, for example, the ministry of women deacons is still a viable tradition. The same prayers of ordination are employed for both the male and female deacon. In the Coptic Orthodox tradition, other prayers for the blessing of a deaconess are used.[13] Paradoxically, in contrast to those many parts of the Orthodox world which are actively engaged in the "academic theory" related to women deacons, the Coptic Orthodox tradition has begun to readily enjoy the ministry of deaconesses even though the theological question regarding their ordination has yet to be officially engaged.

Nevertheless, the participants at the Istanbul meeting were encouraged to reflect more deeply upon this tradition through the welcoming address of Ecumenical Patriarch Bartholomew. He reminded the participants that:

> Since the earliest days of the Church, faithful Christian women and men have lived in this city…Here, at the Great Church of Hagia Sophia a number of devoted women, such as St. Olympias, served as deaconesses.… To both women and men, to both clergy and laity, these women saints continue to be a source of inspiration, for it is written: 'God is revealed in His saints!'

After affirming the Rhodes Consultation, His All-holiness added:

> The order of women deacons is an undeniable part of tradition coming from the early Church. Now, in many of our Churches, there is a growing desire to restore this order so that the spiritual needs of the people of God may be better served. There are already a number of women who appear to be called to this ministry.

The ordination of women as presbyters (priests) and bishops was not brought up at any of the formal or informal discussions in Damascus. This is clearly not an issue for Orthodox women from the Middle East, Africa and Asia. Similarly, the ordination of women as presbyters and bishops was not an issue for the delegates from North and South America, Europe and Russia. At the same time, there was a common appreciation expressed by the delegates that this has become an important ecumenical issue coming from traditions originating in the West.

For this reason, the findings of Professor Constantine Yiokarinis, a theologian from the University of Athens, were included for consideration during one of the panel discussions of Constantinople. After an exhaustive study of Greek patristic texts, Professor Yiokarinis concludes that there is no theological reason why women cannot be received into the presbyterate (priesthood) and episcopacy. He is among a small but growing number of Orthodox theologians who publicly have begun to arrive at this same conclusion.

It will not surprise many to note that the Orthodox generally have been reluctant to engage deeply in official bilateral theological discussions related to the ordination of women. This has been particularly evident since the ordination of women priests in the Episcopal Church in the early 1970's. This reluctance may be starting to change, albeit slowly. The ordination of women was the theme investigated during the historic international bilateral discussions held between the Orthodox and Old Catholic Churches. These took place in Levadia, Greece (1996) and Warsaw, Poland (1997). These discussions are historic because they were the first official bilateral theological exchanges on this topic involving the Orthodox.

After careful examination and discussion, the theologians from both delegations could find no theological reason that would prohibit the ordination of women to any of the three major orders, namely the diaconate, presbyterate and episcopacy. Since these historic discussions, Old Catholics have proceeded to ordain women to all three orders. [14] The findings of the bilateral discussions, nevertheless, generally had not become public during the time of the Orthodox women's conferences.

With the above in mind, it is interesting to note that of their own accord participants organized extra discussion time in order to listen to Professor Yiokarinis' research more carefully. To the surprise of some, over a third of the delegates attended this meeting. At the very least, this phenomenon may indicate that Orthodox women generally may be comfortable considering and discussing this issue with other Orthodox women even when they personally may not be proponents of the ordination of women as presbyters and bishops.

Toward a Renewed Traditional Vision of Ordination and Ministry

All Christians by virtue of their baptism and chrismation (confirmation) are called to "royal priesthood." In other words, at baptism they were "ordained" to the rank of laity. The ancient Christian understanding of the laity as "the people of God," is a body comprised of both clergy and laypersons. Called apart for a particular expression of servant-leadership among the people of God, bishops, presbyters and deacons still belong to and serve as members of the body of Christ. Even as ordained members of the clergy, they do not minister from outside the body of the faithful. In order to reflect our own ecclesiology more authentically, we must resist every temptation to think otherwise.

At the same time, all members of the faithful are within the call to "serve the Church" to the best of their ability. All are called to service in ways that facilitate their relationship with God, other human persons, themselves, as well as creation. Christians are encouraged to discern how they may best extend themselves during every stage of life in a manner that also respects their own personal abilities and needs, responsibilities, and the needs of the community.

Conducting research on the ministry of women deacons required a careful examination of the Orthodox understanding of ordination. That the female deacon is an ordained member of the clergy was first established in this contemporary era during the mid 1940's through the scholarly research of University of Athens theologian, Professor Evangelos Theodorou. The Orthodox at the time tended to be reluctant at first to adopt his conclusions. This is because these conclusions defied a number of preconceptions regarding ordination, ecclesiology and other aspects of theology that had been held at the time.

Through the years, continued thoughtful study and reflection on this and other topics began a shift in realization by many Orthodox theologians. This was the realization that a significant degree of these assumptions were perhaps less dependant upon the witness of the Fathers and Mothers of the Church and more reflective at least in part, upon medieval western scholastic theology.

These faulty assumptions combined with cultural influences and historical circumstances made even some of the most highly respected Orthodox theologians hesitate in examining and accepting Theodorou's findings.

Through the subsequent decades into the twenty-first century, among numerous other endeavors, Professor Theodorou continues his efforts to explore this topic. Today, he is still an active proponent for the ordination of women deacons. Over time, his efforts have inspired other Orthodox theologians to study this issue for themselves. As a result of these efforts, the Orthodox generally have come to accept the fact that deaconesses are ordained; and that this, as well as other theological assumptions regarding ordination, ministry, ecclesiology and authority in the Church have been held "captive," to some degree, to medieval western scholasticism.[15] With the above in mind and in an exquisite manner, the Orthodox may have come to realize the truth of the historic adage attributed to the third century African bishop, St. Cyprian of Carthage: "A custom without truth, is merely an ancient error."

The Ordination of Women Deacons: The "Elephant in the Room"?

All authentic ministries reflect the diversity of gifts given to the Church by the Lord Jesus Christ, Himself, through the Holy Spirit of God. On a deeply spiritual and psychological level, our capacity to respond to the issue of women deacons may be a direct reflection of our maturity in discerning other ministries as well, both lay and ordained. At this point, let us turn our attention back to the concerns raised earlier by women who experience a call to serve the Church through some expression of a visible and dynamic ministry. Some from among this number are also endeavoring to respond to a call to ordained service.

We may benefit here by remembering the observation of Patriarch Bartholomew regarding the possible rejuvenation of women deacons, "there are already a number of women who appear to be called to this ministry." This observation may reveal a heart and mind continuously striving to discern where God is leading His people. This observation may point to a mind and heart sincerely engaged with contemporary pastoral challenges and concerns. This observation may also demonstrate a heart and mind ever seeking to identify a variety of fitting laborers desiring to commit themselves in the Lord's service. This observation is one based in profound love of God and neighbor, not fear.

Unfortunately, some may be turning their eyes and hearts in another direction by trying to avoid the elephant in the room which is how the Holy Spirit of God may be active among His people and calling them to ministry – ordained and non-ordained. In certain situations, vocations are being discouraged as a way to "protect" the Church from considering women's ordination to the presbyterate and episcopacy. In essence, this strategy not only seeks to hold the rejuvenation of the ministry of women deacons but every potential ministry, "hostage." This approach may frequently succumb to using shame and intimidation to enforce a particular human-based *status quo* of ecclesial life that may not faithfully bear witness to Tradition of which is the presence of the Holy Spirit expressed within the life of the Church.

Instead, we would benefit greatly to heed thoughtfully the teaching of St. Paul:

> Now there is a diversity of gifts but the same Spirit; and there is a diversity of ministries, but the same Lord; and there is a diversity of activities, but it is the same God who empowers all of them in everyone. To each is given the manifestation of the Spirit for the common good... (1 Cor. 12: 4-7)

As a result of research and personal experience within the life of the Church, I have come to believe strongly that the Lord God is truly calling certain women to serve Him as His ordained ministers through the diaconate. He is also calling many others to serve Him through other expressions of visible and dynamic vocational lay ministry. The observations and suggestions offered by the Conferences in Rhodes (1988), Damascus (1996) and Istanbul (1997), and elsewhere illustrate the depth and breadth of this need and desire on behalf of the Church. The more this is true, especially when considering those women who are responding in faith to a call to service, then the more we may find ourselves actually grieving the Holy Spirit of God whenever any of us ignore, discount and/or attack the authentic witness of even one of these persons.

I urge those of you who are able and have the desire to study the ministry of women deacons as fully as possible. Not only may this exploration offer you an opportunity to examine more deeply Orthodox theology concerning salvation, ministry, ordination, the Church and ecclesial authority from this particular vantage point, you may be surprised with the same discovery I experienced. This discovery is that the ministry of women deacons is truly of God and because of this, it is exceedingly beautiful! This simultaneously and joyfully bears witness to the greater context of the truth that every service offered by everyone of us that is received by the loving God, is likewise, exceedingly beautiful! [16]

Conclusion: God is Revealed in His Saints

In many ways, the Damascus and Istanbul meetings in particular may serve as a microcosm of the consciousness of the Church. It is especially important to remember here that these conferences were not gatherings of any particular self-selected group. Instead, the delegates were trusted Orthodox Christians chosen by their regional churches to represent them and these women took this responsibility very seriously! They were representative of some of the best the regional churches had to offer. In many ways, their statements provide us with a humble blueprint from which to begin.

Discerning how local churches may implement initiatives based upon the concerns raised by the delegates will depend upon various practical considerations and pastoral needs. Nevertheless, with the above in mind, the ultimate criterion for discernment will be a spiritual one. At this point, it is important to review the earlier observations made regarding holiness. God desires and calls every human person to share in a creaturely manner: in His very same holiness. He alone makes this ineffable gift possible for us. This is the essential reason why we have been saved. We grow in holiness only as we are receptive to the will and love of God for us and progressing in genuine relationship with Him, ourselves, others and creation. In a sense, holiness is for us, a kind of radical and unconditional integrity founded in the life-giving presence of God. It is also a definitive mark of the Church.

Because of this, holiness is still an essential requirement for all ministry whether lay or ordained, male or female. It is *the* fundamental requirement in the early Church for ordination whether for bishops, presbyters, male or female deacons and for the consecration of abbots and abbesses of monasteries. Once vocations were discerned and tested, ministries were gratefully received through the worshipping community. The ability to receive much like the ability to be thankful (i.e., *eucharistia*) is grounded in absolute humility and joyful surrender to the love of the living God.

Today, women continue to seek to serve the Lord through His Holy Church in a myriad of ways. The story of the widow's mite in the Gospel of Luke (21:2) reminds us to have confidence that in the eyes of God no sincere offering is ever too small! Some women may also desire to commit themselves to more active expressions of service. A number from among these persons hope to serve in dynamic pastoral, evangelical and/or apostolic vocational ministries that are appropriate to the laity. Others from within these numbers have already admitted that they are responding to a persistent and fervent desire to serve, even obeying a "call" to ordained ministry. Are we ready to receive the varied and wonderful gift God is sending to the Church today through the person of these women? How may ordained clergy and lay leaders be better prepared to receive this wonderful gift?

Our wisest response reflects directly our willingness and ability to recognize, surrender to and receive the "God who is revealed in His saints."

Notes

[1] St. Athanasius the Great, *On the Incarnation*, 54.

[2] *Women Deacons in the Orthodox Church: Called to Holiness and Ministry* (Brookline, MA: Holy Cross Orthodox Press, 1999)

[3] Terres des Femmes, 1995, cited in *MaryMartha*, Colin Williams, trans., p. 23; The author was also in attendance of this meeting; cf. *Women Deacons in the Orthodox Church*, Kyriaki Karidoyanes FitzGerald, (Brookline, MA: Holy Cross Orthodox Press) 1999.

[4] emphasis added.

[5] *Orthodox Women Speak: Discerning the 'Signs of the Times,'* (Brookline, Holy Cross Orthodox Press and the World Council of Churches, 1999). While I have borrowed directly from this book throughout this presentation of selected themes addressed by these international conferences, the reader is urged to consult the text in order to review the concerns in full.

[6] Even as she lay dying of cancer, to her very last breath, Mother Sophia continued to give instructions to her associates regarding how to utilize their financial and material resources to help those in their care.

[7] For more discussion regarding *sophrosyne*, see: *Women Deacons*, pp. 92-95.

[8] *The Place of Woman in the Orthodox Church and the Question of the Ordination of Women*, ed. Gennadios Limouris, ("Tertios" Publications: Katerini, Greece) 1992, p.9; A third of the invited participants to this Consultation were Orthodox women theologians.

[9] *The St. Nina Quarterly*, 1:4, Fall 1997, p. 20; Deep appreciation is also extended here to Prof. Tarik Mitri who provided an English translation of these decisions.

[10] *The Place of Woman in the Orthodox Church...*, p. 28

[11] Emphasis added.

[12] Patriarch Bartholomew I, "Environment and Religious Education," in *Cosmic Grace and Humble Prayer*, pp. 110-111.

[13] Prayers from the rite presently utilized by the Coptic Orthodox Church, however, include adaptations of the ancient ordination prayer for the women deacon from the *Apostolic Constitutions*, prayers from the Byzantine ordination rite of the deaconess and other sources. The original ancient prayers indicate ordination *(heirotonia)*, in contrast to conferring a blessing or appointment *(heirothesia)*; cf. *Women Deacons*, FitzGerald.

[14] Their findings were subsequently published in German and Greek.

They are now also available in English. See: *Gender and the Image of Christ*, in *Anglican Theological Review*, 2002, 84 (3) Urs von Arx and Anastasios Kallis, eds., Duncan Reid, trans., 485-755. Professor Yiokarinis and this author were among the Orthodox theologians invited to participate at these deliberations.

[15] This is discussed in greater detail in my study on women deacons. Paradoxically, in recent decades, the growing movement for the rejuvenation of the ministry of women deacons in the Roman Catholic Church has freely borrowed from the tradition and theology of the Orthodox. See for example my, "Women Deacons? An Eastern Orthodox Perspective," *Origins*, 35:35, 581-587.

[16] In October 2004, the Holy Synod of the Church of Greece decided to promote women to the diaconate. As of April 2006, thus far no ordinations have occurred. See Appendix.

Appendix

Church of Greece Restores Diaconate for Women*

by Dr. Kyriaki Karidoyanes FitzGerald

The Holy Synod of the Church of Greece has decided to restore the order of the diaconate for women. Under the leadership of Archbishop Christodoulos of Athens, the decision was taken at the October 8, 2004 meeting which brought together 64 bishops from throughout Greece.

The decision was announced the following day on the web site of the Church of Greece and in the Greek paper *Kathimerini*.

The historic decision was made by a majority of the bishops following an extensive discussion. Before their decision, the bishops heard a comprehensive presentation on the topic by His Eminence Metropolitan Chrysostom of Chalkidos. He presented the theological, liturgical, canonical, and ministerial aspects of the order of the diaconate for women.

According to the report of the Holy Synod, Metropolitan Chrysostom concluded his presentation by affirming: "It is certainly possible to rejuvenate this praiseworthy order, with its many diversified and blessed activities, as long as the Church decides this is necessary, after carefully weighing her needs and study, being illumined by the Holy Spirit concerning the 'signs of the times.'"

Archbishop Christodoulos of Athens fully endorsed the presentation and expressed his own support for the rejuvenation of the order. According to the Synod's statement, the Archbishop concluded the deliberations by "affirming the missionary, catechetical, philanthropic and social efforts of women today in Greece. He particularly stressed deep appreciation for women who voluntarily contribute to the betterment of society and emphasized their vital place in the life of the Church."

The restoration of the ministry of the diaconate for women has

---

*As reported in www.orthodoxnews.org

been a particular concern for Archbishop Christodoulos. While serving as Metropolitan of Demetriados, now the region of Volos, he ordained a nun in the year 1986. For the rite, he made use of the ancient ordination prayers of the Byzantine period. Throughout his ministry, he has been a consistent advocate for the restoration of the order.

The Holy Synod's Statement says that the bishops affirmed that "the institution (*thesmos*) of deaconesses established in antiquity and rooted in the Holy Canons was never abolished…" The Holy Synod also say, that depending on opportunities, "the regional Bishop may consecrate (*kathosiosi*) senior nuns of Holy Monasteries of their Eparchy; in order to address the needs of their Holy Monasteries, and only with the understanding that the deaconess is not appointed to the rank (*bathmos*) of priesthood."

Professor Evangelos Theodorou, emeritus Professor at the University of Athens, applauded the decision of the bishops. In a telephone interview, Professor Theodorou stated that the decision initially to receive nuns to the order must be seen as the first step toward fully reestablishing the diaconate for women. He noted that the bishops want to take the restoration one step at a time.

Theodorou believes that eventually other devoted and qualified women will be eligible to be ordained. He feels that this is implicit in the positive remarks made by Archbishop Christodoulos and other bishops at the Synod meeting. Theodorou says "some bishops already have publicly expressed their desire for deaconesses to minister within the wider society on behalf of the Church."

Theodorou also says that the bishops clearly recognized that they were restoring the ancient order which was important in the life of the Church for generations. He believes that the ordination rite of the Byzantine period will be used in future ordinations of deaconesses.

Professor Theodorou's scholarly examination of the history of women deacons was first published in the year 1948. In his monumental study published in 1954, Theodorou clearly demonstrates that women were truly ordained as deacons in the Orthodox Church at least through the Middle Ages, and that the order never completely disappeared to this very day. Based upon an extensive study of ancient sources, Theodorou convincingly shows that women deacons were ordained at the Altar during the Liturgy in a manner similar to male deacons. In his study, Theodorou reproduces the ordination prayers for women deacons used in the Byzantine period. He also identifies and discusses the many responsibilities which women deacons had in the Church.

As professor at the University of Athens, Theodorou was the teacher of many of the bishops who approved the decision to restore the diaconate for women. His historic studies and his many scholarly articles on women deacons are well known to clergy and theologians in Greece, and throughout the Orthodox world. He presently serves as a senior advisor to Archbishop Christodoulos.

The decision of the Holy Synod of the Church of Greece is in conformity with the decision of the Pan-Orthodox Consultation on Rhodes in 1988.

Convened by the Ecumenical Patriarchate, this Consultation brought together representatives of the autocephalous Orthodox churches. There, the delegates also formally reaffirmed that women had been ordained as deacons in the Church. They also noted that the order had never totally fallen out of existence. Mindful of the historical and liturgical evidence, the delegates formally called for the restoration of the order of the diaconate for women to serve the needs of the Church today.

About the Patriarch Athenagoras Orthodox Institute

The mission of the Patriarch Athenagoras Orthodox Institute is to educate, communicate, promote, and sustain the traditions, values, teachings, and culture of Orthodox Christianity. The Institute is a member of the Graduate Theological Union at Berkeley (www.gtu.edu), a consortium of theological schools and centers. The Institute sponsors the Master of Arts with a specialization in Orthodox Christian Studies, education programs for the community, and the Orthodox Christian Fellowship for students of the University of California, Berkeley and the Graduate Theological Union.

The Patriarch Athenagoras Orthodox Institute was established in 1981. It was designated a patriarchal institute by the Holy and Sacred Synod of the Ecumenical Patriarchate of Constantinople in 1992. The Institute is the only center of learning in the United States with this designation.

The Institute established the Distinguished Lecture series in 1988 in order to bring the finest scholars on topics of concern to the Orthodox Church and have them share their research with the academic community of the Graduate Theological Union and the University of California as well as the greater Bay Area. In 2002, the Distinguished Lectures were named for Paul G. Manolis, on the occasion of his retirement after many years as Director of the Institute. Many of the lecture series have been published by the Institute's publishing arm, InterOrthodox Press. For more information about the Institute, visit our website www.orthodoxinstitute.org.

The Distinguished Lecture Series has been delivered by:

His Grace Bishop Kallistos (Ware) of Diokleia

Rev. John Meyendorff

Jaroslav Pelikan

His Eminence Archbishop Methodios (Fouyas) of Pisidia

Sir Dimitri Obolensky

Lydia Black

Christos Yannaras

Kyriaki Karidoyanes FitzGerald

His Beatitude Archbishop Anastasios (Yannoulatos) of Tirana and All Albania

Robert F. Taft, SJ

About the Author

Kyriaki Karidoyanes FitzGerald, M.Div., Ph.D. is an Orthodox theologian, author and licensed psychologist who has studied at the School of Theology of the University of Thessaloniki in Greece and holds a doctorate from Boston University. Her publications include *Women Deacons in the Orthodox Church: Called to Holiness and Ministry, Orthodox Women Speak: Discerning the 'Signs of the Times'* (ed.), *Encountering Women of Faith: St. Catherine's Vision Collection. vol.* (ed.) and *Living the Beatitudes: Perspectives from Orthodox Spirituality* (co-authored with her husband, Fr. Thomas FitzGerald). She has taught at theological schools in Europe and the United States and has represented the Ecumenical Patriarchate of Constantinople on the Faith and Order Commission of the World Council of Churches and at other theological conferences and ecumenical meetings. She participated in the historic Pan-Orthodox Consultation on the role and ministry of women in the Church sponsored by the Ecumenical Patriarchate, held on the island of Rhodes, Greece in 1988. Dr. FitzGerald is the Founder and Coordinator of *St. Catherine's Vision* (www.orthodoxwomen.org), a working group of persons committed to studying and supporting the many ways women and men are called to serve within the life of the Church, today. Most recently, she presented the 2006 Isaac Hecker Lecture at St. Paul's College in Washington, D.C.